THE AMERICAN MARITIME LIBRARY: VOLUME II

WAKE OF THE COASTERS

WAKE OF THE COASTERS

By JOHN F. LEAVITT

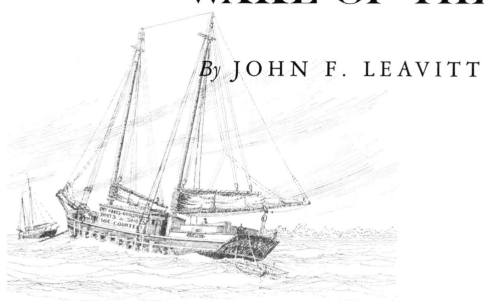

Mystic Seaport Museum, Incorporated

ISBN: 0—913372—34—X

Manufactured in the United States of America

*To my wife Virginia who, through more than forty years
of marriage, has been forced to listen to such yarns over and over,
yet whose encouragement and even insistence is largely
responsible for the completion of this book.*

CONTENTS

ILLUSTRATIONS

PREFACE

THIS book is not intended as a history of coasting vessels nor of the coasting trade. It is a haphazard series of recollections of men, vessels, and ports — of a way of life now vanished and almost forgotten. It is written with some hesitation and misgiving for after half a century one finds it difficult at times to separate the cold outline of fact from the nostalgic images of youth in retrospect.

Therefore I will not vouch for its accuracy in every detail for I cannot after all these years trust my own memory completely, much less the authenticity of all the yarns and "scuttlebutt" gossip I heard so long ago. I have, however, attempted to convey a bit of the flavor of life as I knew it along the Maine coast among the vessels and the men who sailed them in the twilight of the coasting trade.

Those days were the last of an era when skill in handling their schooners and a superlative knowledge of coastal pilotage enabled Maine coastermen to keep the ancient and frequently decrepit survivors of a once vast fleet at sea.

I have not attempted to touch upon the larger schooners of which there were many in those last years. I knew most of the vessels and some of the masters, mates, and crews but their maritime world was different from that of the smaller schooners in which I spent most of my time.

The bigger vessels can safely be left to writers like Captain W. J. L. Parker, whose authoritative work on the New England coal schooners leads us to hope that his talents and tremendous collection of data will be combined to produce a definitive work on the sailing coasting trade as a whole.

Perhaps I should apologize for occasionally attempting the impossibility of reproducing the speech and idiom of the coast. Even after forty years spent largely out of the state it comes quite easily to my tongue but any attempt to convey the flavor of it on paper is probably doomed to failure. However, there are certain pronunciations and expressions that I can not bring myself to "dress up." I only hope I will not be classed with those would-be comedians whose idea of Maine speech is a nasal whine like the braying of a hungry jackass.

Those who already know the coast and the people will be able, I hope, to translate the written word into speech as they read.

Those who have not visited the coast may be inspired to do so in the future, although I warn them they will find few traces of the life of which I write. They may as well go West seeking gun-toting cowboys and wagon trains. Nevertheless, they can come to know that which never changes — the sea, the sky, and the rocky, tree-clad coast. It is there today as it was fifty years ago, unchanged and unchanging. It will be there, God willing, fifty centuries from now with the sea wind whispering through the spruces and the surf still beating against the unyielding rock.

ACKNOWLEDGEMENTS

VERY few enterprises can be completed by individual effort. In my spasmodic efforts to finish this book during the past fifteen years, I have had the assistance and encouragement of many people, loans and gifts of photographs and access to manuscripts and other material to check events and dates which I found, amazingly enough, were not always as clear in my mind as I had thought them to be. Most of them are old friends; others are chance acquaintances; but to them all, I extend my sincere thanks. Those I particularly wish to mention are: John Quincy Adams of South Lincoln, Massachusetts, for his advice and encouragement and for the photographs he was wise enough to take when he was cruising the coast as a boy; Ernest S. Dodge, Director, and the staff of the Peabody Museum, Salem, Massachusetts; Marion V. Brewington, formerly Curator of Maritime History at the Peabody Museum and now Director of the Kendall Whaling Museum at Sharon, Massachusetts; the Peterson brothers, Roland, Murray, and Roger of Arrowsic, South Bristol, and Cape Elizabeth, Maine; Captain W. J. L. Parker, USCG (Ret.), of Camden, Maine; Charles S. Morgan of Concord, Massachusetts; Andrew J. Nesdall of Waban, Massachusetts; Andrew Willis of Boston; Giles M. S. Tod of Hingham; Captain Fred C. Smith of Short Hills, New Jersey; Curator Edmund E. Lynch and fellow staff members of The Marine Historical Association Inc. at Mystic Seaport; and last, but not least, Captain Francis E. "Biff" Bowker, master of the schooner *Brilliant* and, like myself, an alumnus of the sailing coasters.

WAKE OF THE COASTERS

1 | THERE WAS A TIME

Riding along the coastal roads of Maine, I catch myself now and then looking eagerly toward the waterfront as though expecting to see the spars of a coasting schooner rising above the trees or a long jibboom thrusting out from behind a tumble-down wharf house. Disappointment is inevitable for, except a few survivors operating as "dude cruisers" out of Camden or Rockland, the day of the sailing coaster has come to an end. The dude cruisers are only maritime ghosts in an atomic world and bear exactly the same relationship to reality as dude ranches do to the old West. Their holds, once redolent of lingering scents of past cargoes, now smell of perfume and shaving cream faintly tinged with bilge water. Instead of tiers of lumber or carefully chocked blocks of granite, there are accommodations for the schoolmarms, bank clerks, and secretaries who make up their paying crews.

There was a time when spars and rigging made a commonplace pattern against the Maine sky. It was in 1938 when the last cargo-carrying coaster was launched in the state of Maine, yet today there seem to be very few who remember when the reaches and thoroughfares swarmed with coasting schooners. Perhaps that is because the sight was so taken for granted. On the other hand, until the advent of good roads in the middle to later 1920s, most of the isolated towns east of Portland depended upon the schooners for connection with the outside world, particularly during that part of the year when the dirt roads were nearly impassable. For all the years since Maine had become a state and even before, much of her economy was built around shipping, both deep water and coastal. It took thousands of men to build and man the vessels, to load and discharge their cargoes, and the arrival of a coaster in any down-east harbor was an event welcomed by all. After a long icebound winter, a schooner nosing her way around the point was a sight to gladden the hearts of many. It was as though communication with the rest of the world had been re-established.

The years immediately following the First World War found survivors of the coasting fleet busy although their numbers were diminishing inexorably. No one seemed to foresee the inevitable end for there were still millions of feet of lumber, tons upon tons of granite and many other cargoes to be transported to the westward economically in coasters.

There were many then who remembered the halcyon days at the height of the coasting trade when a statistically minded keeper at Owl's Head light tallied the vessels sailing by his lofty perch guarding the westerly approach to Rockland Harbor and Penobscot Bay. During the year 1876 he counted over 16,000 schooners alone not including sailing vessels of other rigs or steamers. Many were counted over and over again, so the figures are not indicative of the number of vessels engaged. They do convey an idea of the volume of maritime traffic in the Penobscot Bay area.

Optimism touched the people of coastal Maine just as it did everyone else when the First World War came to an end in 1918. The fighting was over; the world was safe for democracy, and everyone assumed they could return to the old way of life secure in the knowledge that the days of wars were ended with peace and prosperity stretching endlessly before them.

There had been a postwar slump in deep water shipping and the wharves of Boston and New York and the back coves of Maine were the refuge of big schooners tied up and waiting for cargoes that never seemed to materialize. This had little effect, however, on the coasting trade carried on by the little two- and three-masted schooners hailing from the ports of eastern Maine. A few small coasters were actually built in the first few years after the war while others were rebuilt and refitted.

As the words of the old deep water chantey went, "Times were hard and wages low . . ." but most coastermen optimistically looked for improvement. Meanwhile vessels could be operated profitably if expenses could be kept sufficiently low. Certainly wages and grub bills were at the irreducible minimum. Most of the schooners were sailed by two- or three-man crews, depending on the size of the vessel. The master, more frequently than not, was owner also and at least one of the crew was likely to be a son or a close relative. Wages were anything from $30 to $50 a month depending upon whether the deckhand, or mate, as he was sometimes called, doubled as cook. If a third hand was carried he was usually a boy whose wages were only $15 or $20 a month and occasionally even less.

Since the small coasters were never long at sea, the food was usually fresh and fairly plentiful, although of the cheapest variety. Inexpensive cuts of meat and fish could be had from stores at a cost of a few cents. To this day, one of my favorite meals, as an old coaster hand, is salt fish and potatoes worked into a tasty hash with plenty of crisp pork scraps and a little fat. In those days a giant slack-salted pollock could be had for pennies, and few coasters went to sea without one or two hanging from a nail behind the galley stove. There it might grow black and absorb the odor of wood smoke but that only enhanced the flavor. It could be freshened out to suit any taste and a strip of it was a favorite morsel on which to chew between meals.

All hands provided their own blankets and bedding, a thin "donkey's breakfast" made of cheap ticking and straw being available for a couple of dollars in any waterfront outfitting store. Occasionally an adjacent hayfield would be raided for a more fragrant mattress. The bunks were no more than wooden troughs and it was easy in summer to fill them with fresh hay and change it whenever the opportunity afforded.

Bedbugs and cockroaches were sometimes a problem but seldom in a vessel where the skipper's wife was along. As a matter of fact they were never as prevalent in the smaller schooners as they were in the larger vessels. Most of the masters and crews were "home-towners" accustomed to reasonably clean living at home and, while many a shore-bound wife would have been horrified at some of the cooking and housekeeping aboard a coaster, it could have been much worse. On occasions it was, for there are always those bound to live in a state of filth and these made seagoing slums out of their vessels. One old skipper took not only his family to sea with him but his livestock as well. The former forecastle of his old packet, vacated when the deck hoisting engine replaced the larger crews, was a combination pigpen and henhouse, and the schooner was generally referred to as the "floating barnyard." It was claimed she was recognizable in a fog by the smell.

The cabin in any schooner could get rather musty after being kept closed for long spells during bad weather, but with a whole world of fresh air just outside it was a simple matter to air it out. In anything but the worst weather, the after quarters were a pleasant retreat.

There was little formality of the sort found in deep water ships, and the master, usually known as the "old man," lived exactly as did his crew. He might have a stateroom to himself or a choice of bunks, but otherwise he fared like everyone else. He expected his orders to be obeyed, but the aloofness and reserve of the average deep water skipper was seldom found in the masters of small coasters.

The greatest single aid to short-handed operation was un-questionably the gasoline hoisting engine. This was usually installed in the forward deckhouse, if there was one, and, if not, under a box or cover of some kind adjacent to the foremast. The favorite was the Fairbanks Morse "Bulldog," a one-cylinder, two-cycle machine which was as powerful as it was noisy. These engines were hooked up in various ingenious ways to windlass and pumps, and also operated two winch heads at the ends of a horizontal shaft on which the halyards were wound when hoisting sail or lifting out cargo.

Most coasters were equipped with an old-fashioned log windlass, hove around by hand brakes hooked to ratchet gears. In most cases even after the windlass was hooked up to the hoisting engine by a sprocket chain and ring gear fitted around the barrel, the hand gear was retained. The windlass was invariably set just aft of the big samson post at the heel of the bowsprit. The rocker arm for the hand brakes was mounted on the forward side, and the iron-shod windlass pawl on the after face of the post.

The anchor chain, coming in through the hawsepipe beside the knightheads, encircled the barrel of the windlass in three round turns and was tiered in a box or grating on deck if there was no chain locker below. When anchoring, the chain had to be overhauled and flaked down on deck ahead of the windlass so that it would run clear when the anchor was dropped from the cathead. Once the anchor was on bottom more chain was payed out simply by lifting the last turn from around the barrel and heaving it forward. If the vessel was straining hard on her chain it could be a ticklish job to keep one's fingers from getting mashed or one's clothes from becoming entangled in the leaping chain.

Setting sail with a hoisting engine was a simple process for a couple of men. The peak and throat halyards led through large footblocks shackled into U bolts in the waterways abreast of each mast. Snatch blocks were hooked into ringbolts or pendants in order to give a fair lead to the winch heads when the halyards were led through them. The mainsail was set first and then the foresail, the latter having its sheet well overhauled to allow it to swing free while the headsails were being hoisted. Once the sail was stretched and the halyard was "two blocks," one man clapped a stopper on each halyard in turn at the footblock, holding it with one hand and taking the turns on the belaying pin with the other as the halyard was released from the winch head forward.

It was often simpler and as fast as or faster than using the engine to hand hoist the headsails, for it was essential to make the vessel's head pay off as soon as the anchor was off bottom. The simple process of hand hoisting a sail is a more skillfully coordinated performance than the average landsman would guess. Two men face each other, each with his hands on the halyard, left hand close above left hand; with their right hands they reach for the next hold above their heads. This has to be done with perfect coordination, with the weight of their bodies brought down in unison. Done properly, it is a graceful operation to watch and one that is surprisingly difficult to perform without practice.

Chanteys were not sung in coasters, at least in the later years, but men frequently "sang out" when hoisting or hauling by hand. Hoisting hand over hand like on a jib halyard, one might chant in rhythm, "*Hey* yah, *ho* yah, *up* yah, *down* yah!" and repeat until the sail was hoisted. Actually, the words were usually indistin-

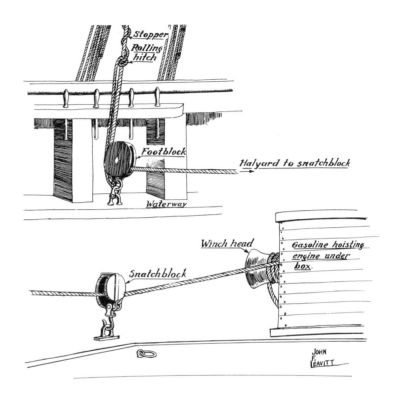

1. Peak and throat halyards were almost invariably led so, snatch blocks being located in various places to ensure a "fair lead" to the winch heads. The stopper was necessary to hold the halyard once the sail was hoisted so it could be released from the winch head and made fast on the belaying pin adjacent to the footblock.

guishable syllables and might be anything at all as long as a pattern of rhythm was provided.

Working at windlass brakes the cadence was much the same, although for long or short "drags" it could be paced to suit the occasion. This was a far cry from the wild chanteying of a gang of Liverpool "packet rats" who "blew the man down" or "paid Paddy Doyle for his boots." It accomplished the same purpose, however, and was a pleasant sound to hear across the water as "all hands and the cook" tailed away on the halyards of a big "hand puller" or hove smartly on the windlass brakes.

The jib was customarily set on a boom that extended along the foot of the sail, but in some vessels, particularly those originating on Long Island Sound and waters further south, a 3- or 4-foot "club" was used instead of a full-length boom. The clew of the sail was often cut off diagonally to take it, and the sheet block was fastened midway of its length. The club was commonly called a "skull cracker" by the down easters and it deserved the name. Theoretically, the sail set better but in beating to windward, it flogged wildly every time the vessel came about and was a constant menace to anyone forward.

Topsails were set and clewed up from the deck, although it was necessary to go aloft to cast off the gaskets or make them fast as the case might be. Once the gaskets were cast off, the next step was to overhaul the clewline and then man the halyard. The luff of the sail was bent to wooden hoops, and since the canvas was of lighter weight and smaller size than the lower sails, it slid easily up the topmast. Next, the sheet was manned and the clew hauled out and down to the end of the gaff. In setting a topsail, the sail was always set to leeward of the peak halyard, but the tack was hove down to the weather side of the gaff and carried around the mast to be made fast on the pin through the leeward boom jaws. It was not shifted on the main when tacking, but the fore topsail had to be either shifted or furled each time the schooner came about because of the spring stay. With short-handed crews in later years, this task became a nuisance, and consequently most of the smaller schooners either did not carry a fore topmast or never bothered to set a sail on it. To clew up a topsail, the sheet and tack were cast off the pins and the clewline was manned, bunching the sail at the topmast head. Most of the small vessels had the clewline running around the leech and foot of the sail, leading from the head down to the clew and then along the foot so the sail clewed up in a bag. Big schooners usually had their clewlines rove through a wooden bull's-eye worked into the belly of the sail to act as a spilling line, which made it somewhat easier to clew up a large topsail by spilling the wind out of it. In a small vessel, there were usually two or three bull's-eyes or lizards on the leech and foot of the topsail through which the clewline was rove. Once the sail was bunched at the topmast head, the halyard was cast off and the sail brought down to the masthead by hauling on the clewline. It was then necessary to go aloft, work the sail into a neat bundle, and pass the gaskets to hold it close to the mastheads.

In bad weather, furling and gasketing the topsails could be quite a chore and occasionally it was necessary to take the clewlines to the winch head. Most skippers made an attempt to clew up light sails before bad weather really set in, but now and then they were caught by squalls with heavy rain or snow. At such times,

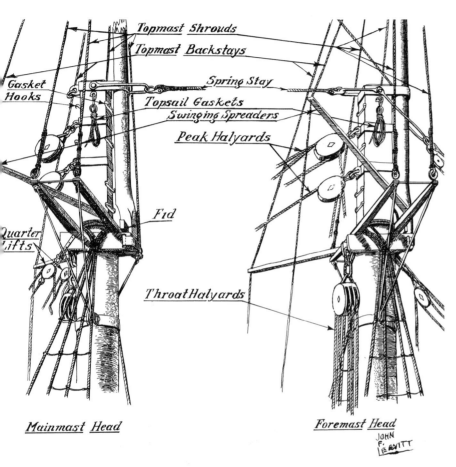

Topmast Shrouds
Topmast Backstays
Gasket Hooks
Spring Stay
Topsail Gaskets
Swinging Spreaders
Peak Halyards
Fid
Quarter Lifts
Throat Halyards

Mainmast Head

Foremast Head

JOHN F. LEAVITT

2. Details of masthead gear on a two-masted coaster. There were many variations but this is fairly typical.

working aloft to furl rain-sodden or sleet-stiffened canvas was a rugged job, but it was always a one-man operation in the smaller schooners. In the later years it was a tiresome process if a fore topsail was set, for it meant furling and gasketing one and then either crossing from mast to mast by way of the spring stay or descending to the deck and climbing aloft again. Furling a topsail, however, was not so bad as in square riggers where one worked on a footrope with "one hand for the ship and one hand for yourself." In the schooners there were the crosstrees to stand on and the topmast shrouds behind one's shoulders to give some protection from falling outboard. Often there were gasket hooks on the forward and after sides of the square mastheads, and once the topsails were close-furled, it was a simple job to lace the gasket back and forth from hook to hook.

Most youngsters liked to cross from mast to mast via the spring stay. It saved going back down to the deck and up again, but if there was any sea running, it was an adventurous journey. The masts worked to a surprising degree, and the stay alternately sagged and stretched with a snap that put quite a strain on the arms and wrists when a man was dangling by the hands.

In good weather, working aloft was a pleasure. If there was a fore topsail, it was often considered not worthwhile to set it, and at such a time the sail could be arranged inside the slackened gasket to make a perfectly comfortable "crow's nest." I have spent countless pleasant hours there on summer days reading or just watching the motion of the schooner as she shouldered her way lazily through the swells, scattering broken water from the bow and leaving a trail of bubbling froth to mark the wake.

Once off Portland I sighted a giant shadow not far ahead, deep below the surface of the sea, and shouted a warning to the old man at the wheel. He promptly assured me there wasn't a ledge within miles. Sure enough, the "shadow" rose to the surface and, breaking water, proved to be a big finback whale. With some anxiety I recalled stories of whaling vessels stove in by attacking cetaceans. This one, however, seemed not disposed to commit any form of mayhem and after swimming companionably alongside for a few hundred yards, took off for Davy Jones' locker again in a smother of foam and with a farewell flirt of his tail as he dove out of sight.

The only really unhappy experience I ever had aloft was once coming out of Boothbay Harbor in the *M. M. Hamilton,* when the old man decided I should do something useful like slushing down the newly scraped main topmast. We had a tremendous deckload of boxboards, and in the deep ground swell off the Cuckolds the schooner was rolling heavily, her spars swinging in a wide arc across the sky. I wasn't keen about the chore, but in coasters, as in deep water ships, it was a case of "growl you may but go you must"; so taking a bucket of the thick yellow grease we called "slush" and a bo's'n's chair, I set out for the masthead. Reaching the crosstrees, I shackled the bo's'n's chair to the topsail halyard block and gave the signal to hoist away. Up I went to the topmast head some 90 feet above the water. Holding fast with one hand I began slapping grease on the bare topmast with the other. Due to overconfidence in my capacity for hard cider at a dance the previous evening, I was not feeling up to par and before long my stomach gave indications of rebellion. I yelled down to ask them to lower me away but the skipper shouted back to stay where I was until the job was finished. Before I could convince him of the necessity for descent, it was too late. There was not too much wind and since I was twisted around facing aft my breakfast landed in the belly of the mainsail, some of it spattering down on the old man at the wheel. After that I didn't dare come down, for the skipper's dissertation on my ancestry, intelligence, and habits was a masterpiece of vituperation which lost little of its force on account of distance.

In most small coasters the main hatch was located midway between the two masts, or further forward if the vessel was a centerboarder. In such schooners the centerboard usually extended from the after edge of the main hatch to the smaller hatch aft of the mainmast, the mast being stepped off center to clear the case which extended by it. In schooners built for the lumber trade the hatches were larger, and in the stone trade the coamings were higher and the hatch located as far aft as possible. In the earlier days lumber schooners were invariably built with bowports in the hull through which timber or long lumber could be loaded. Long lumber such as ship timber or spar stock could only be worked into the hold through these ports, and it was often rafted alongside and loaded from the water. Once loaded, the ports were heavily braced and caulked so there was no chance for leakage. A vessel which consistently loaded in fresh water, however, soon developed rot in her bow structure due to the fresh water which soaked the adjacent timbers as the lumber was pulled dripping from the river and dragged in through the bow ports.

The after deckhouse, which in later years almost invariably

3. Loading long lumber or piling through bowports was a wet, dirty, and backbreaking job and was the cause of much rot in the vessel's bow structure.

4. Flush after houses were not uncommon, for they allowed much more room for the quarters below. It was something of a nuisance, however, to get from aft forward or vice versa.

housed the entire crew, was about 12 to 20 feet long depending on the size of the vessel and as wide as possible, leaving narrow walkways or quarter-alleys between the house sides and the quarterdeck railing. Occasionally a coach house or door opened directly onto the main deck from the forward end of the cabin, but the main entrance was usually down an after companionway on the port side from the quarterdeck. In some schooners the after houses were carried out flush to the sides of the hull, which gave excellent accommodations below and a high poop over which the old man or the watch officer could pace in serene pomposity. Such arrangements were usually found only in the larger two-masters and some of the three-masters. Several of the Ellsworth vessels including the *Lavolta,* the *Storm Petrel,* and the *Henrietta Whitney* were so arranged, as was the big *Sarah Eaton* from Calais and the *Cameo.* In all these vessels, the hands slept in a forward house.

In most schooners the quarterdeck or poop was the same height as the main rail and ended at the forward end of the after house or just forward of it. Some were extended well forward of the mainmast, but not often in the small vessels unless it was carried all the way forward to become a "riz" deck, meaning a deck flush all the way forward or to the fore rigging at the height of the main rail. In such cases a small open "well" deck was left for the windlass and its gear, and from the break, aft, the "riz" deck was enclosed by an open or fly rail on turned stanchions. Many packets and most vessels in the lime trade were so rigged. In a few instances the quarterdeck ended halfway along the length of the after house and was only half the height of the main rail. It was designated as a "boot heel" and was usually seen only in very old

5. Looking aft on the main deck of a small coaster, showing one of the two water barrels and a pump as well as the steps to the quarter-deck.

vessels. Some schooners brought down east from Long Island Sound or the New Jersey area had the low quarterdeck about half the height of the main rail, always carried to the forward end of the house or forward of the mainmast. A few were flush decked fore and aft; these were almost invariably smaller vessels such as the Hudson and North River "brickers" and a few refugees from the Chesapeake.

In the later years the most important equipment aboard, aside from the deck hoisting engine, was the power yawl-boat that hung from the stern davits. The name, which had nothing to do with the sailing rig known to yachtsmen, originated in the days when a yawl was a ship's boat of smaller size that hung on stern davits. In down-east coasters it was always called the "yawl-bo't." Any small sailing craft was usually called a "sloop-bo't" or occasionally a "schooner-bo't." The word "bo't" was used to designate almost any small craft, whether propelled by oars, sail, or engine. The word is almost unpronounceable to people other than those brought up on the Maine coast. The "o" is short — not long as in "boat" but not yet like the "o" in "bought"; about halfway between the two is the best way it can be described. The same pronunciation is applied to words like "road," "coat," and "spoon."

To get back to the yawl-boats. They were heavily built, carvel-planked, transom-sterned boats, originally for rowing, but after the introduction of gasoline engines for marine use, they were almost invariably powered with a one-cylinder, two-cycle "make and break" engine, known colloquially as a "one lunger." These machines were very simple as engines go and possessed amazing efficiency and power for their size. They turned a big pro-

6. The *Morris & Cliff*, "riz" deck lime coaster, typical of vessels engaged primarily in that trade. The deck was carried forward at the height of the original main rail, ending at the forward house. It was enclosed by an open or "fly" rail and afforded more dry stowage for casks of lime.

peller at slow speed, and although rated at only five to ten horse-power, the "horses" were all Percherons, for they would push a hundred-ton schooner along at a good clip, even if the vessel were deep-loaded and bucking a head tide or current. Using a yawl-boat was called towing, which was perhaps not the proper term to describe the function, since they actually were for pushing, and in fact were occasionally referred to as "push-bo'ts." The craft was lowered into the water from the stern davits, and the falls were hooked into a becket in the bow, which was then hoisted up so its padded stem came against the schooner's transom. Single lines were run to each corner of the yawl-boat's stern as quarter guys, and the engine was started. There was no clutch or reverse gear and to stop the engine it was necessary to throw the battery switch. After running for a long time, the engine got really warmed up to its work and often continued to fire even after the switch was thrown. The first time this ever happened to me, I had come all the way across Portland Harbor from Peaks Island roads. Heading into one of the Portland wharves where there was a landing stage, I waited until too late to cut the switch and when the engine continued to fire happily for a few more revolutions, I ploughed bow-on into the float stage, springing the stem of the boat and putting a V-shaped dent in the float. I fell over backwards with legs waving in the air, much to the edification of a few spectators. The engine's idiosyncrasy could prove even more embarrassing if it occurred when one was trying to shove a schooner into a crowded dock. I recall hearing of one skipper who was heading up a wharf at the head of which stood one of those little edifices made famous by the late Chic Sale. His engine continued to fire and he missed a

cast with a dockline, creating a debacle that left the outhouse a heap of boards after the schooner's bowsprit plunged through it. The way to reverse the engine was to pull the switch momentarily and throw it back again at the proper time to catch the piston between strokes. This caused the engine to backfire and run in reverse.

With the boat pushing away under the stern, steering was done by the schooner's wheel, and tows of several miles at an average speed of 3 to 4 knots were nothing unusual. Vessels slated to load their cargoes far up some river or narrow bay got there much more easily by yawl tow than they used to in the days when they had to wait for a fair wind and tide or be "kedged up" by hand. This operation involved running a long line and kedge anchor out ahead and hauling the vessel up to it. But even in the days of power yawl-boats, there were some rivers where the current was strong enough to make it necessary to "tide up."

In the later years most coasters sailed only with a fair wind and frequently spent days at anchor waiting for a "chance along." At times, however, the more ambitious with a destination in sight to windward hauled up hard on the wind and beat their schooners in, although it could be a long and exhausting process. Some of the centerboarders worked well to windward in smoother water, but the vessels without boards were slow in stays and frequently had to be "box hauled" in the process of tacking if they were beating up a narrow waterway. In such cases it was tack and tack all the way. The schooner would be no more than filled away on one tack with a good "rap full" than the old man would sing out again, "Ready about!" One man stood by the head sheets forward while

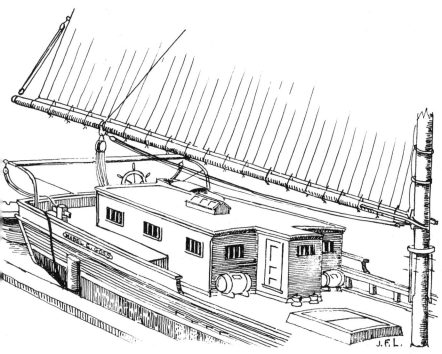

7. "Boot heel" poops were not too common but some of the older vessels had them.

the other ran aft to the poop. There he clapped a heavy watch tackle to the main boom bail from a ringbolt on the weather side of the deck. The skipper then eased the helm down, calling out "Hard alee!" as he did so, warning the man forward to let fly the head sheets. Slipping a becket on the wheel, he then jumped to the aid of the hand on the watch tackle and together they hauled the main boom to windward. This gave added impetus in bringing the vessel's head up and across the wind, particularly since the headsails were no longer full. For a few minutes there was a wild flogging of canvas and loose gear as the vessel came into the eye of the wind. The tail rope of the big jib had been made fast to leeward and as the wind came on the other side this sail, being aback, made her swing even faster. The hand aft raced forward again and as the schooner payed off on the other tack, it was a fast, two-man job to get the big headsails flattened in and drawing. The jib tail rope was cast off (drawn away) and slammed across. The leeward tail rope was then made fast in readiness for the next tack. If there were additional headsails, it was a real workout to get them trimmed and made fast before they "took charge." There was just about time to get the gear coiled down and made ready when it was time to do it all over again. The maneuver was insurance against misstaying, for the old saying was "She's got to tack or break in the middle!"

If there was plenty of sea room, such maneuvering was unnecessary. Then it became a simple matter of easing the helm down and sailing her in a wide half circle from tack to tack. Very few coasters would stand an attempt to snap them from one tack to another. If there was room, it was usually best to lay them off a little just before tacking to get a good full and have the vessel moving. The helm would then be eased down gradually, and unless she was unusually balky she would sail around, keeping good way from tack to tack. Some of the big multimasted schooners used to wear around if there was enough sea room, but seldom was the maneuver necessary for the smaller vessels.

Sailing up to or away from a wharf was not an unusual procedure. The vessels were slow and clumsy when compared to the average yacht, but the skippers knew them well, and I have seen some pretty handling in docking a schooner under sail or getting underway from the wharfside. Most vessels carrying lumber to the Maine Central pier in Rockland were sailed in to or away from it as long as the wind served. We even did it in the old *Lulu W. Eppes* and she was as hard to handle as any vessel of her size on the coast. Captain Freeman Closson sailed her in as though he were coming alongside in a twenty-footer instead of in an 80-ton coaster that sailed and worked like a sand barge. Many of the Portland packet schooners used to sail in to Widgery's wharf, and with several of them strung out in a line along the wharf it was a pretty piece of work to watch as one more came sliding in to put her docklines ashore with a minimum of commotion.

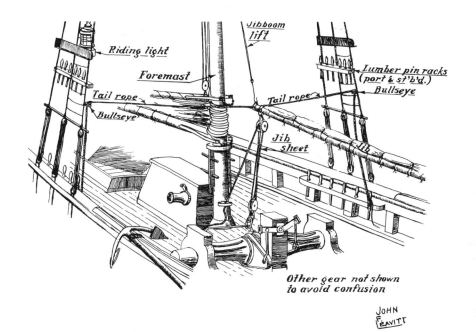

8. The tail rope was an important piece of gear when beating a coaster to windward. Once the vessel filled away on a tack, the lee tail rope was made fast, thus holding the big jib to windward when the schooner came about again. It was "drawn away" (let go) once the vessel was on the other tack.

PHOEBE MARIA

JOHN
LEAVITT

2 | THE WAY OF LIFE

IT seems incredible that in a few short years a traditional way of life once existing along the coast has completely vanished. Like the frontier days and cattle drives in the West, or the era of clipper ships and hard-driving masters in the Cape Horn trade, it has passed into history.

Life in the coasters was not romantic as it was in the big clippers and the later Cape Horners. The little coasting schooners were no more than seagoing tipcarts, hauling their prosaic cargoes from one coastal port to another. Without them, however, the country could hardly have been settled. Yet they have passed unnoticed and are all but forgotten.

It was an enjoyable way of life for those who could appreciate it. Just as farmers talk of crops and fishermen speak of catches, so did coastermen talk of vessels and cargoes. The entire Maine coast was one vast neighborhood in which every schooner was as familiar as the house next door, and the men who sailed them were as much neighbors as the town dwellers who discussed local gossip across back fences. Just a glance at the sails of a schooner hull down on the horizon served to identify her to any coasterman.

With several coasters anchored in company, ship visiting was a common way to end the day. Often it blew too hard or perhaps not enough to keep the schooners at sea, and several of them would come driving or drifting into any harbor of refuge along the coast as the day waned. Smoke curled from the stovepipes as supper was prepared, and before long skippers and crews appeared on deck for a breath of air and a look at the weather. If it was a pleasant evening, yawl-boat engines might start to pop, and soon several masters and hands would be congregated aboard one vessel or another discussing weather, freights, and mutual acquaintances. The skippers had the seats of honor in the middle of the group, while the hands perched around the deck wherever they could find room. Once the gossip of the day had been disposed of there were often fascinating stories of the history of the coast. The topics of conversation, although confined almost exclusively to vessels and affairs along the coast, seemed to be endless, and to a green boy, new

9. Towing with a yawl-boat down astern is really a simple process. The name of the vessel is fanciful — a whim of the author's.

to the life, it was like hearing the original version of a seagoing *Arabian Nights.*

One would say, "Wonder what happened to Ralph Merriam in the *Railroad* today. He was comin' down from Nor'west Harbor this mornin' jest about th' time I come out o' the thoroughfare. I come over under th' land cal'latin' to pick up more breeze in th' Muscle Ridge but he kep' outside down through Two Bush. I looked for him jest before I come through Davis Strait and he was well outside so I guess he wa'nt comin' in here. Must have kept right on for Portland."

"Yup," another might chime in, "he prob'ly did. Runnin' packet y' got to keep movin'. Y'ever hear 'bout the time Freem Closson was in th' *Lois M. Candage* runnin' freight and grain to Bluehill? Seems his wife was goin' with him . . ." and so it would go, one yarn leading to another. Seamen love to "talk shop" and coastermen were no exception to the rule. Politics, family affairs and, inevitably, women, received a measure of attention but sooner or later the talk always turned to vessels, crews, and ports. Lively debates were carried on regarding the relative sailing capabilities of different schooners and their good or bad points in handling. Like all seamen since the days of the Phoenicians, coastermen were quick to defend the reputation of the craft in which they sailed and the arguments often included the merits or demerits of vessels manned by relatives. Information on loading ports was exchanged, and absent skippers or crews were always subjects for gossip, although seldom in critical fashion.

All coastermen found their primary interest in life in their vessels and the trade in which they were engaged. To many, the schooners were simply the means to make a living, but to others, they were far more.

Brought up along the coast, most men's lives had the tendency to fall into the patterns established by those who had gone before. It was the only way of life they knew and they carried it on, conforming as their fathers had done and learning as they had learned. It was essentially a different form of sea life from that experienced by those who went offshore. Because it was carried on almost entirely within sight of land and in almost constant communication with the coast, it was never quite free of some of the ways and viewpoints of the landsmen. There was seldom the complete severance of shore ties, the identification "with" the sea and the sense of being "of" it. Perhaps because the land was so near, men perforce depended more upon it and thought of it as the ultimate objective of the passage rather than thinking of the passage itself. There was pride in a good passage; pride in the vessels, but not quite in the same sense that is felt by men whose landfalls lie thousands of miles away on the other side of the world. Offshore seamen live their lives in the ships and ports are merely interludes between voyages. On the coast the ports are important, and the passages are generally regarded as simply the process of getting from one place to another.

On the other hand, there were times when the vessel, the weather, and the opportunity combined to produce a passage delightful to experience and memorable to look back upon. Sometimes it might be only a short run of a few miles from one harbor to another around the next cape. Again it might be a night passage across the Gulf of Maine with a fair wind over the quarter, or a beat up the coast in company with another schooner which became an absorbing race as long as it lasted. There was, for instance, the day of the long beat up against a smoky sou'wester in the *Eugenie,* splitting tacks with the *Regina,* both of us having sailed from Boothbay in the morning bound for Boston. I am sure neither master thought of a "race" when we sailed, but by the time we tacked in company off Seguin, each had determined to keep on as long as the wind held, even though it was almost a "dead muzzler." We kept the schooners hard at it and found ourselves becoming critical of the set of the sails and the steering. Soon we were trimming sails in an effort to get the most out of them, and when we tacked offshore we were quite even although the *Regina* was somewhat to windward of us but slightly astern. We were both lumber laden and both of the same rig, although *Regina* had something of an edge on us in the matter of size.

The wind freshened as the day wore on, and in no time the spray was flying in sheets over the deckloads of both vessels. Both had main topsails set and, as we watched, a jib topsail crept up the stay to the *Regina's* fore topmast. Frantically we went rummaging in the lazarette, hoping to find a sail to match. We did, although it was gray and mildewed in spots and didn't look as though it would hold a cap full of wind. We bent and set it, however, and miraculously it held. The *Regina* had gained on us and was now as far to windward and somewhat ahead. Offshore we went, topmasts and flying jibboom bending to the pull of the sails and the loose gear flying in bights. Sant Lloyd at the wheel nursed the *Eugenie* carefully up across the steep crested seas, taking advantage of every little puff that let the schooner steal a few feet to windward and holding her to it when she shouldered into a curling sea that exploded into showers of spray leaping high above the weather bow. A mounting wave hissed along her lee quarter, some of it tumbling inboard and the rest breaking into froth as it merged with the wake astern.

With the coastline dimly blue in the distance, Captain Wallace tacked the *Regina* and went tearing in on the port tack. Deciding our only chance lay in picking up even more wind offshore, we kept the *Eugenie* at it until we could barely make out the sails of the other vessel in under the land. At last we tacked to stand in, and made out the *Regina* standing off to meet us on the starboard tack. Steadily the two vessels drew together, and although we knew she should be able to cross us we hoped we might have picked up enough on our offshore jaunt to turn the tables. Rapidly the schooners closed and the *Regina* made a grand sight, the sun shining through the sails and the white water breaking around the bow and leaping off the lee side. We had picked up some lost ground, undoubtedly, but at the last moment we had to bear off and go under her stern. Keeping *Eugenie* on the inshore tack only a little longer, we put her about once more and went plunging offshore hoping to do better the next time. Wallace, however, seemed to feel his best chance lay in the waters along shore and proceeded to make a series of short hitches. Well offshore, we tacked in again at last and this time as we converged, we had him. It was close and when we slid ahead of him on the port tack, his jibboom end wasn't 10 feet from our quarter rail as we passed. We could see Emery Wallace's face clearly, and the grizzled old veteran didn't turn a hair as they went boiling astern of us, but Sant Lloyd couldn't resist a grin in response to my obvious delight.

So it went, all through the long day until nightfall found us rolling along in a dying breeze. We had paid for a few miles to westward with more than twelve hours of hard sailing but it had been well worth it. We had done all we could by the vessels and they had responded like two old champions, meeting to compete in a final supreme effort before settling back into the comfortable pace of old age.

Seamen everywhere have always been prone to regard their vessels as animate, and coastermen were no exception. I have heard a hard-headed and unsentimental skipper mumbling words of encouragement and approval as his vessel seemed to take heart and go roaring along on the wings of a fair wind. I have heard him complain bitterly when she acted like a contrary girl and missed stays.

Perhaps it was because we used the right terms of endearment to flatter the lovely little *Abbie S. Walker* that she took us one wild night from Boston Lightship to Mt. Desert Rock at an average of slightly better than 10 knots — a prodigious burst of speed for a little 190-ton three-master, even though she was flying light and fresh off the marine railway. It was like the last great performance of a fading but still beautiful actress, however; not long afterward she made her final exit from the world of waters, going missing with all hands in a winter gale.

Oddly enough, despite the fact that sailing ships have always been considered to be of the feminine gender, despite names or trades, women aboard vessels have always been considered to be bad luck personified. This superstition was never so strong along the coast as it was off soundings, and it was not uncommon for the wives of coasting skippers to accompany their husbands for a few trips now and then, if not all the time.

Some like Bertha Closson or Mrs. Fred Hutchins made floating homes out of their husbands' schooners. Others, of the henpecking type, asserted themselves and made life miserable for all hands. This was usually done indirectly, for not many captains' wives, whether dictatorially inclined or not, ventured to question their husbands' decisions openly. However unwillingly, they bowed to the tradition that the master of a vessel gave all the orders and was the seagoing arbiter of destiny for all aboard. Downeast women, nevertheless, are noted for being able to show disapproval in ways not involving verbal protest. One old skipper found this out after he had been lured into spending a large portion of his hard-earned freight money on a grand but rather inglorious spree in Boston. He was giving a somewhat rueful account of his activities to a group of fellow captains at a loading wharf down east a couple of weeks later. His grimly disapproving spouse was uptown shopping, and it was the first chance his friends had had to ask questions. Finally, one of them inquired, "What about the old woman, Charles, what'd she say?"

"Say?" snorted Cap'n Charles, "She didn't say nawthin' — in fact she ain't said nawthin' for more'n two weeks!"

3 | BE YE BOUND THAR?

SOME coasting skippers were always a little timid (a euphemistic synonym being "moderate") especially in winter weather, and it needed only a darkening of the sky and a shriller note in the wind to send them scurrying for shelter in the nearest harbor to leeward. In later years no one condemned the practice for the vessels were old, and getting caught out in a "hard chance" at night, overloaded and undermanned in a schooner that was just about able to keep afloat, was no picnic.

In an earlier day the smarter masters looked with some contempt on those who always clung to the coast looking for the next harbor. There was a story frequently told by coastermen which illustrates the point. I heard it about Captain Dunbar Grafton of South Cushing, Maine, who was for many years master of Dunn & Elliott's big two-topmaster *Seventy-Six* out of Thomaston.

It seems that once when the *Seventy-Six* was laid up for repairs, Captain Grafton was asked to fill in as mate in another Thomaston schooner whose master was one of the "moderate" kind. His mate had left without warning and the schooner was loaded with lime and ready to drop down river, bound for New York. Heading offshore for Cape Cod it began to look as though bad weather was in the offing, and the master soon showed signs of uneasiness. The wind was in the easterly quadrant; it was winter and the idea of getting too far away from the land didn't appeal to him. Captain Grafton, although temporarily only second in command, had the reputation of being a smart master and something of a "driver" who never let a little bad weather interfere with making a good passage. Therefore, the master of the schooner hesitated to seek shelter unless it became obviously necessary. Finally, his caution got the best of him and he said somewhat tentatively, "Mr. Grafton, it's gettin' kind o' black out there t'th east'ard. Mebbe we better ease her off for Portland." Grafton was pacing up and down the deck and didn't even reply. This was a little discouraging, and it was quite a while before the skipper tried again. "Mr. Grafton," he said, "it's lookin' worse 'n it did and I cal'late we ought to think about gettin' into Portland." Still there was no answer and with a decision one way or the other necessary at once in order to make it, he tried again. "Mr. Grafton," he said, "it don't look like a good chance along to me and I cal'late to keep

10. The *Anna Sophia* — big, clumsy, and slow. Authors' collection.

her off for Portland. Wha' d' you think?" Grafton merely shifted his quid, spat over the lee rail, and drawled, "Be ye bound thar?" The schooner was kept on the course for Cape Cod.

In the last years of coasting, however, few schooners ventured to stay outside except during the summer months when there was a steady fair wind. Most of them lay at anchor for days at a time waiting patiently for a "chance along," and there was hardly a harbor from Kittery to Calais where at least one or two coasters weren't sheltering for the night or riding out a bad spell of weather.

Occasionally, a sizable fleet gathered and on the next clear morning when the wind came off nor'west, there was a symphony of coughing donkey engines, clicking windlass pawls, and squealing blocks while slatting canvas thundered in the freshening breeze. Chain sheets rattled against wire stays as the headsails were sheeted home, and soon a procession of schooners streamed out of the harbor, lifting their bluff bows to the deep ground swell with the green water gurgling and gushing in and out of the hawsepipes and scuppers.

Westerlies had a way of dying with the sun, however, and most skippers preferred to work their way along the coast ready to seek shelter as the night came on. I well remember one of my later trips when a dozen or more schooners came out by the Cuckolds from Boothbay on the wings of what appeared to be a promising nor'wester. There had been a long spell of bad weather and a large fleet had assembled, one by one, but with the clearing shift, we all got under way together. Soon we were strung out in a line,

the bigger schooners leading the way with several little packets and bay coasters bringing up astern.

In the van was the big two-topmaster *Lavolta* and close behind her the *Storm Petrel,* both of Whitcomb, Haynes & Whitney's Ellsworth fleet. We, in the *Gilbert Stancliff,* were a close third, and behind us came the comparatively new stone drogher *Anna Sophia,* built by Lyman Pushee at Dennysville in 1923. She was supposed to have been designed by Captain Ben Paschal, her first master, who had long experience in the stone trade. She was reported to be a failure in that trade, however, and Paschal left her after making only a trip or two. At this time, her skipper was Captain George Eldridge of Machias. His son Carroll was a good friend of mine, and according to him, his father didn't think much of the vessel's working qualities.

Most of the fleet, with the exception of some of the packets and bay coasters which were bound to Portland, kept pretty well bunched during the day, and when it became apparent there would be more dirty weather in the offing, most of us hauled up for Kittery, a familiar harbor of refuge for coasters bound to the westward.

The *Lavolta* and *Storm Petrel,* both laden with stone and bound for New York, went offshore obviously intending to make for Cape Cod and go down over the shoals the next day. Captain Eldridge in the *Anna Sophia,* also stone laden, decided to follow suit, and the last we saw of the trio, they were hull down offshore driving hard through the heavy seas that were beginning to make up.

11. The *Lavolta* of Ellsworth — able, fast, and comfortable. Courtesy
Peabody Museum, Salem, Massachusetts.

The rest of us straggled into Kittery and anchored in the lee of the ledges off Frisbie's wharf with plenty of chain out to hold us against the rising wind. Some time during the night we were joined by the *Anna Sophia.* Next morning when Carroll Eldridge and I got together ashore to compare notes, I learned the vessel had lived up to all of Cap'n George's forebodings. She had proved to be slow and clumsy and wouldn't tack or work well, so it hadn't taken the old man long to decide to wear around and run back for the shelter of Kittery. There we all laid for several more days when another clearing nor-wester scattered the fleet. We later heard that *Lavolta* and *Storm Petrel* had rather a rough time of it, but both were powerful, well-found schooners, and they came through with flying colors.

The *Lavolta,* a 200-ton vessel, was built at Ellsworth in 1870 for Captain John Whitmore who had her in the West Indian trade. She originally had a short poop and a well deck with high bulwarks but was later rebuilt with a raised deck carried all the way forward at the height of the main rail, enclosed by a fly rail on turned stanchions. Her afterhouse was flush to the sides like several other Ellsworth schooners. She was a good sailer, and very few vessels of anywhere near her size could take her measure, particularly in heavy weather. Her skipper for some time in later years was Morris Whittaker, succeeded by Captain John Lowrie, and at last by Captain W. C. Bellaty, formerly in the *Nellie Grant.* For many years she carried staves to New York and usually returned home with coal from Rondout on the Hudson, but in later years was often dispatched for Newtown Creek in New York with granite from Hall's Quarry on Somes' Sound, Sullivan, and other quarry ports. Because of her size, she carried a somewhat larger crew than many two-masters, having a mate, two hands, and a cook besides the master.

In the late twenties, *Lavolta* was laid up as business dwindled and at last she was bought to be converted into a replica of the Puritan ship *Arbella* for the tercentenary celebration of the founding of the Massachusetts Bay Colony. The conversion was done at Salem, and in a few short weeks all resemblance to the handsome, tall-sparred schooner had disappeared. The *Arbella* was taken to Charles River Basin for exhibition and later on returned to Salem where, after further strengthening, she was put into a permanent berth in the Pioneer Village, a city-sponsored tourist attraction. During the ensuing years, she was visited by thousands of people, but in 1955, after showing signs of advanced deterioration, she was broken up.

The *Storm Petrel* was only slightly smaller than the *Lavolta.* For a number of years "Skip" Mazrall had her until he retired to bay coasting in the old *J. Chester Wood* and handed the *Petrel* over to Albert Closson, formerly in the three-master *Winchester.* The *Storm Petrel* had been distinguishable by a solid "box" rail that enclosed her long "riz" deck, but in the twenties there were signs of extensive rot around her waterways and she was rebuilt with an open fly rail.

In the later years, Captain Closson and his brother, Freeman, late of the *Lulu W. Eppes,* went two-handed in her for a few trips to New York, but after getting caught on the Shoals, deep loaded with coal, during a winter gale, they left her. She was sold to New York owners and foundered at sea about 1930.

The *Henrietta A. Whitney,* third of the company's trio of surviving schooners, was originally a two-master named the *E. & I. Oakley,* built further down east. She was badly burned out in the early nineties at Ellsworth, and Whitcomb, Haynes & Whitney bought the wreck and had her rebuilt by Isaac Grant, a third mast being added at the time. The work was extensive, and she was launched in 1895, newly documented and named for Mrs. John O. Whitney, the partners having drawn lots to choose the name. The *Whitney* was actually a smaller vessel in length and beam than the *Lavolta,* but she registered 217 tons, slightly more than the two-master. Her best-known skipper was Captain Johnny Jordan of Ellsworth, who went in her until she was destroyed by fire at Eastport in 1924. She was grounded out alongside a wharf that caught fire, and since she could not be moved, there was no way to save her. Captain Jordan went in other vessels for a time and then took to yachting. Later still, when he was well along toward his eighties, he went in Frank Swift's "dude cruisers" at Camden. He finally retired to his home in Ellsworth and in his nineties made regular trips downtown.

Captain George Robbins of Stonington, Maine, formerly in the *Annie & Reuben* and the *Mary E. Lynch,* had the *Gilbert Stancliff* when I was in her. The *Stancliff* was a 117-ton two-master, built at Middletown, Connecticut, and launched in 1869. She had been extensively rebuilt from time to time, the most recent job having been done about 1919 following a serious grounding in Fox Island Thoroughfare. She was a powerful vessel and a good sailer, although in her last years she was a little too "loose" to stand as much driving as Robbins would have liked to give her.

For a keel schooner of her type, however, she was surprisingly good to windward, and we beat her up Muscongus Sound to Round Pond one trip, boxhauling her every tack but she made it in grand style.

She had come down east early in her career and for many years was owned in Machias and Addison. Just about the time of the First World War, Captain John Stevens of Rockland bought most of her shares and went in her until he sold her to buy the *Lavinia M. Snow.*

George Robbins owned a substantial interest when he was in her later on, but he finally sold out and the *Stancliff* wound up under Nova Scotian ownership. In her last years she had more than her share of trouble. On one passage from Nova Scotia for Boston with a cargo of lumber, she sprang a bad leak and became waterlogged. Her cabin was completely washed out and all stores were lost. Fearing that she might break up, the crew left her but later reboarded and worked her into Mispec, New Brunswick, where temporary repairs were made pending a more extensive job at Rockland.

12. The *Gilbert Stancliff* after launching in 1869. Courtesy Captain
W. J. L. Parker.

4 | DAY ON THE COAST

DAYS at sea, along the coast, are similar in routine yet at the same time infinite in variety. Only ashore are boredom and monotony the companions of one's leisure hours. Even anchored in a harbor with nothing to do but wait for a fair wind, there is a content unknown to those who live their lives on terra firma. Most seamen have learned to walk humbly before the Lord, accepting the pattern of life as they find it. Thus they are free from many of the tensions and restlessness that frequently haunts those who dwell ashore.

In the years I spent on the coast I was, on occasion, cold, hungry, scared, and downright unhappy, but never bored once we were free of the land. Glad to get ashore at the end of a trip, yes — but gladder to haul in the last dockline and see the span of water widen between the schooner and the wharf as she left the land behind and headed for open water.

Even waking in the morning is different from what it is ashore. There is no struggling up uncomprehendingly from the maze of sleep, sodden and bewildered. Wakefulness comes, slow or fast, with the dawn, and with it, the pleasant awareness of familiar sounds and smells. There is the muted lapping of water against the hull and the hum of wind through the rigging. If there is much wind, the slapping of the halyards against the mast and the rumble of the taut anchor chain tells of it. The lingering scent of wood smoke mingles with the smell of pine and spruce lumber, spiced with a whiff of Stockholm tar from the oakum and marlin stowed in the lockers.

It is the boy's job to stir the fire in the stove to life and to put the big coffee pot of water on to boil. This is done, and after sloshing plenty of cold water over one's head, the water bucket has to be filled from one of the barrels on deck and more wood split to keep the fire going hot enough to bake the biscuits which the mate, who also doubles as cook, is making.

The old man climbs the companionway steps for a squint at the weather. He finds it clear and a fair wind making up. Dropping back into the cabin, he reaches for his clothes, observing, "Dry no'theaster, boys — it's a good chance along!"

Meanwhile, the smell of wood smoke mingles with the aroma of frying cow beef and boiling coffee. The coffee will be stronger than love and blacker than sin, but that first cup tastes like nectar brewed for gods on Olympus. Eggs sputter and pop in the frying pan, and the opening oven door allows the escape of the tantalizing fragrance of baking saleratus biscuit. The mate says, "Come and get it before I throw it out!" and we do.

Breakfast is zestfully but rapidly finished, and while the dishes are being safely stacked in the big dishpan wedged tightly into a corner of the counter, the donkey engine is started and the pumps are tried. From our pumps there is only a brief gush of water before they "suck," but aboard the old Calais lumber drogher astern of us, the clanking pumps are not stilled for half an hour or more. There, two men work steadily at the hand pumps, and the engine pump also is pouring water down the deck to mingle with the streams from the after pumps and run overboard through every scupper and freeing port.

Meanwhile, our halyards are led forward through snatchblocks, clear for hoisting, and as they are wound around the winch heads, the spasmodic popping of the donkey engine flattens into a steady rhythm as the mainsail starts aloft amidst the squealing of blocks, the clicking of mast hoops, and the slatting of canvas.

Once the mainsail and foresail are set, the foresheet is well overhauled and the windlass manned. Link by link the chain creeps through the hawsepipe, the pawls clicking in measured cadence until the report, "Anchor's hove short!" is shouted aft to the old man who stands at the wheel.

His reply is immediate. "Break her out then. We'll pay off on the port tack. Don't forget the tail rope!" The answer is, "Port tack it is, Cap'n. Tail rope's all fast."

Once more there is the clink-clink of windlass pawls, this time in increased tempo, and suddenly there is a yell from forward. "Anchor's broken out, Cap'n." A wave of his hand suffices for a reply, and the chain rattles through the hawsepipe faster and faster once the anchor is off bottom.

Windlass brakes are deserted, and there is a rush for the jib halyard. The tail rope from the jib to the weather forward shroud is fast, and as the sail fills, it snaps like a rifle shot in the freshening breeze. Once the jib is hoisted "two blocks" the flying jib is set and sheeted home. Slowly at first and then more swiftly, the schooner pays off and gathers headway. The skipper sings out, "Draw away," and the tail rope is let go. The jib slams across to leeward and the two of us turn again to the windlass brakes.

Shortly the anchor appears through the welter of white water under the bow, and it's " 'Vast heavin' " on the windlass. The "fish hook" on its long pendant is dropped over the bow and hooked into the ring of the anchor. The "burton" or "fish tackle" is hooked on, and once again the rhythm of the snorting "h'ister" smooths out as one man takes the hauling part to the winch and hoists away while the other slacks the chain as the anchor is hauled aft and up to the cathead. The chain lashing is passed and made fast and the fish hook disengaged from the ring. It is slid down the shank to the flukes and the strain is taken on the winch once more. A long handled wooden "fluke spade" is worked under the fluke to prevent it from digging into the planking as it is hoisted inboard. Up it comes until the flukes slide in over the buffalo rail where a chain lashing is passed to hold it fast.

Once the anchor is catted, the next job is washing down and

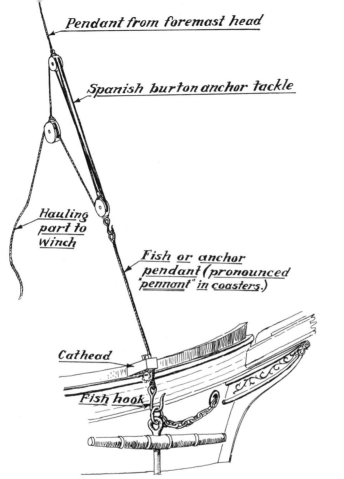

Pendant from foremast head

Spanish burton anchor tackle

Hauling part to Winch

Fish or anchor pendant (pronounced "pennant" in coasters.)

Cathead

Fish hook

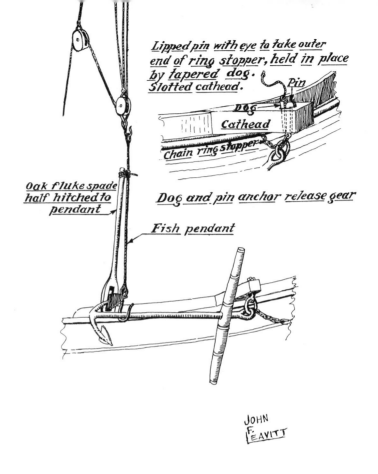

Lipped pin with eye to take outer end of ring stopper, held in place by tapered dog. Slotted cathead.

Pin

Dog

Cathead

Chain ring stopper

Oak fluke spade half hitched to pendant

Dog and pin anchor release gear

Fish pendant

JOHN F. LEAVITT

13. Once the anchor was hove up to the hawsepipe, it was brought to the cathead as indicated in the drawing. The Spanish burton tackle hung permanently from the foremast head and could be used on either side of the vessel. The fish pendant and hook and the wooden fluke spade were stowed along the bulwarks when not in use. The cathead release gear shown is one of the more popular forms. To let the anchor drop, the tapered dog was pulled out and the lipped pin knocked back into the slot with a maul or hammer.

coiling the gear. With a draw bucket sea water is scooped up from overside and sloshed forcefully over the decks, beginning forward where the mud and slime from the anchor chain is drying on the deck. This is done not only for cleanliness but for preservation. Fresh water soaking into wood is one of the primary causes of rot and deterioration around a schooner's deck, and frequent washing with salt water does much to offset them. It also keeps the deck tight as well as washing away the accumulated harbor dirt and grime.

The halyards are coiled down on deck directly in front of the pins on which they are made fast. Lighter gear is sometimes made up in a small coil and hung over the belaying pins but the halyards are not. They are kept free for running, the coil loose and the loops clear of each other so they will not foul when the sail is lowered away. In big schooners the halyards are often wound on reels in the rigging but there is not room for this in the smaller vessels.

In the meantime, the mate has gone below and when he reappears on deck he brings the coffee pot and three cups for a final "mug-up" before cleaning and refilling. In a coaster the coffee pot is always on the stove, winter and summer, at all hours of day or night.

The old man at the wheel has been casting an appraising eye aloft, and he drawls, "Hey, Jack, get a ball of marlin and put a new servin' on that splice in the for'ard end of the spring stay. It's come adrift and you might as well fix it now. While you're up there, you can cast off the gaskets on the tops'ls. We may want to set 'em if the breeze holds the same outside." Dropping below I get the marlin, a small serving board, and a spike and start for the fore rigging. The old man yells after me, "While you're up there, take a look at them seizin's on the topmast shrouds and fix 'em up too if they need it."

By this time the schooner is bowing more and more deeply to the increasing swells that come rolling in through the outer channel. The breeze is freshening and dollops of spray explode against the taut canvas like charges of bird shot.

We are the first schooner out and behind us trail the others, one of them a smart little three-master overhauling us steadily, as with her tall rig she drives through the fleet. She passes us just as I reach the fore crosstrees and I brace myself between the masthead and the topmast shrouds to watch her go plunging past, close enough so we can hear the creaking of her gear. Her old man is also at the wheel and he waves a casual hand as they go thrashing past. His crew pause in their tasks to wave, all with elaborate unconcern. We wave back, trying to appear nonchalant and disinterested but secretly we are crestfallen and envious. We know we can take the measure of any two-master anywhere near our size and it galls us to play second fiddle even to a swift three-master like the *Mattie J. Alles*.

The other schooners are unable to gain on us and two of them are dropping further behind, so I turn to my job after casting the topsail gasket adrift and taking a few turns with it around my waist. On a job like this it is simpler to lash one's self to the masthead and leave both hands free to work with. The task takes the better part of two hours, for it is done in leisurely fashion in order to prolong the pleasure of working aloft. By this time the outer buoy has been cleared and we gybe over, taking the wind well aft on the starboard quarter to slide up by Bass Harbor Head. The four-part main boom tackle has been hooked into its wire pendant leading aft from the fore rigging, thus eliminating any possibility of a standing gybe, for the wind is pretty well aft and approaching Bass Harbor bar, the seas get steeper and the rolling more violent. The wind is steady, however, and the dark islands are etched in sharp silhouette against a clear sky. The sun, rising toward the meridian, turns the water into a blazing cascade of diamonds spilling down over the dancing wave crests, and way up in the rigging the view is magnificent as we sweep by the lighthouse looming high above the water on the heavily wooded shore. The keeper deserts his morning polishing chores in the tower to watch us go by, and his wife appears on the porch of the house to wave her broom in salute.

At last the job aloft is finished, and after crossing over to the mainmast head via the spring stay to cast off the main topsail gasket, I descend to the deck, and the mate and I set both topsails. The mate takes the wheel while the skipper perches moodily on the quarter rail, sucking away on his gurgling corncob pipe. Going below, I put away the marlin and the tools, wash and stow the dishes, and, pouring a cup of coffee, retrace my steps to the quarterdeck. The old man and the mate reject my offer to get them a cup, so I finish mine and clamber to the top of the after house to bask peacefully in the sun, lying on my back to watch the topmast trucks swing in rhythmic pattern across the sky.

Fetching the bell off Black Island, we run through York Narrows, and I take over the wheel when the mate decides a dried apple pie would taste good and goes below to prepare it. Settling myself on the wheelbox, I prepare for a long session of steering. The skipper sits unmoving, wrapped in his own thoughts, and there is only the humming of the wind through the rigging, the creaking and slatting of gear, and the gurgling of water in the rudder port beneath where I am sitting.

Up through the dogleg channel we wind our way toward the eastern entrance of Deer Isle Thoroughfare, taking in the boom tackle and clewing up the fore topsail lest the constant changes in heading necessitate a gybe. Going through the thoroughfare, we meet one of McLoon's sardine carriers bound east, her crude oil engine pounding out a rhythm familiar everywhere along the coast — "ker whump, ker-whump, ker'whump." These old "c.o.'s," as they were called, were almost the standard power plants for downeast carriers and smacks and were recognizable everywhere by the sound. All along the coast, in bright weather or thick fog, the thumping exhaust heralded the approach of such vessels.

Passing Crotch Island we see the *Annie & Reuben* and the *George R. Bradford,* one already loaded with stone and the other about to be. Across the waterway at one of the Stonington town wharves, the *James A. Webster* is lying, apparently deserted for the time being.

With the fresh breeze still holding, we cross the bay and enter Fox Island Thoroughfare. In this landlocked passage, the wind is lighter and we ease through, meeting the *Henry H. Chamberlain* just luffing up to anchor off the town of North Haven. She is flying light bound east, and there isn't much sense in trying to beat her through the thoroughfare.

Once out in Penobscot Bay the old man says, "Keep her down for Fisherman's Island Passage. We'll go into the Muscle Ridge and gybe over when we get in under the land."

In the clear weather the passage entrance can easily be made out only a few miles ahead of us. The sea is a little more "hubbly" now and the schooner begins to dance along in livelier fashion. She is harder on the helm and no longer is it possible to sit easily on the wheelbox steering with one hand. However, it is beautiful sailing; the view up the bay is magnificent and the smell of freshly cooked pies wafted up the companionway is a promise of good eating to come.

At this point the skipper comes over to take the wheel saying, "You'd better get the gear overhauled for'ard. We'll be gybin' over 'fore long." He hollers down the companionway at the mate who shortly appears on deck. I go aloft to make sure the fore topsail gear is well overhauled and the sail snugly bunched below the spring stay. It has hung in the gear since we took it in after coming through York Narrows, and I take a few turns with the gasket to keep it snug when we gybe over.

Running into the Muscle Ridge Channel we meet the lime schooner *Mary Langdon* coming down from Owl's Head, deep-loaded and bound to the westward. Passing under her stern, we stand a little further inshore before the skipper sings out, "Stand by to gybe!" The mate goes aft to tend the mainsheet while I stand by forward. Without further ado the old man rolls the wheel hard up and as the vessel begins to swing off the wind, the mate takes in the slack on the mainsheet and catches a turn with it on the quarter bitts, as the big mainsail swings across and fetches up with

a crash on the other side. I trim the headsheets and coil them down again. The old man decides not to bother with the topsail so there is nothing to do but watch the closing of the gap between ourselves and the *Mary Langdon*. She is by now ahead of us, but soon we go sliding past her.

By this time, dinner is ready, late but all the more welcome. The mate takes the wheel and the skipper and I eat together. Beef stew with dumplings (a little soggy but tasty), a pan of saleratus biscuit, and most of one pie disappear from the table, largely as a result of my appetite, for the old man is not a heavy eater. Gulping down my last cup of coffee I ascend to the deck and take over the wheel while the mate does partial justice to his own cooking. I enjoy the wheel while I can, for steering is always preferable to washing dishes and that chore faces me when the meal is over.

The wind is lightening as we slide along the coast by White-head, Tennant's Harbor and Mosquito Island. Passing Whitehead, we give a blast on the foghorn and out of the keeper's house comes a small figure racing down over the rocks to the big fog bell. Reaching up to grab the lanyard on the clapper, she (it's the keeper's small daughter) swings on it, and across the intervening water comes the sonorous clang of the neighborly salute.

Once clear of Whitehead we look to the westward to see the spars of a pair of three-masters loading stone at Long Cove. The outer one we make out to be the *Charles H. Klinck,* but the other behind her is half-hidden so we can not be sure of the identification, but it looks like the *Annie B. Mitchell.*

By the time we fetch Mosquito Island, it is almost calm and we barely have steerage way. The old man decides that if there's

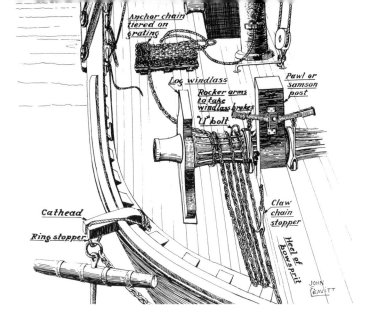

Anchor chain
tiered on
grating

Log windlass

Rocker arms
to take
windlass brakes

"U" bolt

Pawl or
Samson
post

Claw
chain
stopper

Heel of
bowsprit

Cathead

Ring stopper

JOHN
LEAVITT

14. Starboard side of the forward deck of a small coaster, showing how the chain was ranged out in preparation for anchoring. There were, of course, many variations in arrangement and equipment, but that shown in the drawing is quite typical.

going to be no more wind than this, he'll lay over in Port Clyde and hope the breeze will come up with the sun next day.

Outside, the ground swell still breaks against the disintegrating hull of the concrete steamer *Polias* on the tip of the Old Cilley ledge, and behind us the *Mary Langdon* plows doggedly along in our wake, but she is a long way back. The bell buoy clangs half-heartedly in mournful fashion, and a horde of gulls screams and fights over the gurry thrown overboard from a fishing sloop heading in for Port Clyde, her one-lunger banging away in

irregular rhythm. Drifting in by Marshall's Point we see we are not to be alone. Phil Billings is there in the *Clara B. Kennard*, and the *E. T. Hamor* is also anchored, deep-loaded and apparently waiting for a chance along to the eastward. There are several fishermen tied up to the town wharf and a big smack is taking on a load of lobsters.

We are getting close in and it is time to overhaul the chain and make ready to anchor. Putting a "claw" stopper on the chain, several turns are hove forward over the barrel of the windlass and flaked down fore and aft beside the bowsprit. With as much chain overhauled as there is room for in the limited space, the U bolt is inserted in its holes in the windlass barrel over the running part of the chain. This will prevent overriding turns and consequent fouling. The lashing on the fluke is cast off and the anchor pried up and dropped to swing clear at the cathead. Jib and flying jib halyard coils are taken off the pins, and all other halyard coils checked to make sure they are clear for lowering away. The main topsail is clewed up and the sheet and tack overhauled to be sure they will not jam when and if the mainsail is lowered.

By this time we are well into the harbor and ready to round up. The mate and I stand by forward and the old man eases the helm down. Slowly but steadily the schooner rounds into the wind and we let the headsheets fly. At a wave of the skipper's hand we cast the halyards off the pins and, manning the downhauls, bring the headsails swiftly down the stays. The foresheet is also cast off and overhauled so the sail will swing free as the vessel comes into the eye of the wind.

Still we forge ahead a little and with most of the turns off the anchor lashing at the cat head, we await the signal from aft. At last the forward motion ceases and imperceptibly the vessel begins to make sternway. From the old man comes the order, "Let go!" Off come the last turns and the big anchor plunges to the bottom, the chain roaring over the windlass barrel and out through the hawsepipe to fetch up at last with a jerk that seemingly threatens to tear the windlass from the deck. More and more chain is fed over the windlass until the 15-fathom shackle is at the water edge.

Once the anchor is down, we turn our attention to the foresail, and with one man at each halyard we cautiously lower away, keeping a full turn around the pin. If the halyard gets away from you there is hell to pay, for it is almost impossible to catch another turn once it has started to run, and any attempt to hold it is almost sure to result in mangled hands.

With the foresail down, the old man decides to let the mainsail stand overnight. It looks like a calm night and we can always turn out and lower away if it breezes on later. We take in the mainsheet taut as possible and clap a watch tackle on from the bail on the main boom to a ringbolt at the side of the deck and set it up hard. Going forward again, we furl the headsails and pass the gaskets, one man to each sail, and then the two of us put stops on the foresail which is hanging in the lazyjacks. Loose gear is coiled on the pins and the pumps are tried, but a few strokes is all we get before they suck. A becket is put on the wheel and, as a precaution, I go aloft once more to take a couple of turns with the gasket around the main topsail bunched loosely at the masthead.

With everything snugged down for the night there is nothing to do except wait for supper and hope the skipper may decide to put the yawl-boat in the water and go ashore or go visiting, but he doesn't seem disposed to do so. After supper he takes a turn all around deck for a last look at everything while I light the big riding light and hang it in place in the fore rigging. The *Mary Langdon* comes drifting in, her red and green running lights throwing lances of color across the calm water. The wind died out on her almost completely and she has been a long time making the last few miles. She rounds up under our stern to anchor abreast of us, and for a while the stillness is broken by the clacking of blocks and later the clanking of pumps. At last, with a final caugh and a rattle from her donkey engine, the sound dies away and peace descends on the harbor once more. Ashore, a dog barks briefly, but soon, he, too, is still.

For a while the mate and I sit aft talking quietly while the moon creeps high in the sky, touching the broad roofs on the wharf buildings with silver. The trees that surround the town and the spars of the vessels are silhouetted against the sky, and here and there the riding lights and the few lights ashore wink like fireflies. A vagrant night wind begins to whisper faintly, and once again there is the chuckle of water against the hull and the drumming of halyards against the mast. Suddenly the bunk seems like a very pleasant place to head for, and in no time at all, I settle back onto my straw-filled mattress, beneath the old army blankets. The skipper is already snoring lustily, and I wonder how long it will take me to follow his example. Resolutely I ignore the sound and concentrate on the day's events. It was a good chance along . . . hope tomorrow is as good . . . I'm more tired than I thought . . . I wonder . . . and at last, I fall asleep.

15. The *Lavinia M. Snow* at "home" where she was built. Courtesy
Captain W. J. L. Parker.

5 | ROCKLAND AND THE BAY

In the twenties, the Maine coast was an enchanting place for a boy whose principal interest in life was ships and the sea. The day of the down-east Cape Horner was long over, but there were many surviving masters, mates, and seamen still living along the coast. Everywhere there were schooners, either active or laid up. Weathered hulls littered the back coves of many a harbor, and wrecks of all types were to be seen at tumble-down wharves and in lonely backwaters.

Outside Port Clyde, the hulk of one of the concrete-hulled U.S. Shipping Board steamers, the *Polias,* loomed high on the outer end of the Old Cilley ledges. For many years she was the immovable object against which the irresistible surf hammered unceasingly. She had hit the ledge doing a good 10 knots and remained there. Her nameboards and other material from the wreck showed up years later in antique shops all along the coast. Several abortive attempts at salvage had been made, but it soon became apparent that she was there to stay.

She was still there when I sailed through Two Bush channel one of the first times in a coaster. It was one of those melancholy days when there was a bite in the air, and the sky, sea, and trees along the shore were dark before the final clearing of the southeast gale that had driven us down from Boston. Astern, above the shrill piping of the wind and the crash of seas surging inboard over the lee rail, we could hear the cadenced moaning of the whistling buoy on the Old Man ledge. Inshore a white ridge of foam rushed out along the reef and burst in a smother of spray that leaped high over the bridge of the broken ship. Above the sound of the wind came the keening of hundreds of wind-tossed gulls, swooping and gliding over the wreck as though mourning the passing of another stout vessel.

Later the weather moderated and cleared as we sailed into Penobscot Bay. One's first view of the bay should always be from seaward if possible. Distance lends enchantment and the detail of towns along the shore is lost. They are dwarfed by the magnificent range of hills that form their background, and they seem like toy villages. The high land ranges far up the western shore to the entrance of the swiftly flowing Penobscot (called the Bangor River by most coastermen), and across the bay lie the islands of Vinalhaven and North Haven, blue in the distance. They are the Fox Islands and separating them is the winding waterway known as Fox Island Thoroughfare. Heavily wooded Long Island and its smaller satellites stretch up the wide expanse of water toward Cape Rosier. On a spring or summer day when the cloud shadows drift in dark patches across the wooded hills and cleared fields, and the water blazes with light where the sun strikes the wave crests, it is doubtful if even the famed Bay of Naples could more delight the eye of the beholder. It was probably from these hills that Edna St. Vincent Millay looked to see the "three long mountains and a wood" of her famous poem *Renascence.* Here indeed the sky stretches high above the world to give some intimation of infinity.

Once ashore there was little of poetry in Rockland itself, but the long waterfront in those days was never dull. Down at the south end there was a tangle of spars above the buildings at the shipyard of I. L. Snow & Co. Schooners large and small were tied up at the wharves or hauled on the railways for repair. In the backwater behind the yard all kinds of hulls in various stages of disintegration could be seen. Blackened keels and frames showed above the mud, and hulls with spars gone and decks fallen in lay with the tide flowing in and out of the empty holds. There were others not too long since at sea, but now abandoned because the owners could not or would not pay for repairs.

The old *Caroline Gray,* once a West Indian trading brig, later a schooner, and lastly a mastless barge, squatted in the mud stubbornly resisting the inroads of rot, worms, and general deterioration. In later years the three-masted schooners *George Klinck* and *Charles Klinck* leaned helplessly against the piling until they were finally rescued from retirement by the demands of wartime transportation.

In the early twenties the Snow-built schooners *Helvetia, Lavinia M. Snow, Wawenock* and several others could occasionally be found tied up at the yard like children come home for a visit. The big railway was seldom empty, for it was about the only hauling ways suitable for big vessels east of Portland. Here could be seen any type of craft from a Finnish bark to little bay coasters like the *Joyce Rebecca* or the *Ella Eudora.*

A few hundred yards along the waterfront to the north, the Maine Central pier thrust its length well out into the harbor. Two spur tracks, one on each side, extended to the outer end, passenger cars on the south side and freight cars on the other. Several steamboats took passengers from the train and conveyed them to their ultimate destinations on the islands or to the various little towns further along the coast not served by the railroads. The freight trains took the loads of boxboards, stone, and other cargoes brought by the schooners from loading ports equally remote. The trains were backed down from the regular station uptown for the convenience of passengers and to enable freight to be loaded directly from the vessels. Occasionally, fashionable and fastidious ladies waiting in boredom for the bay steamers strolled across the wharf to gaze disdainfully at the "dirty old boats." Little did they think that in another decade or so the same vessels would become quaint reminders of a bygone era and that people would be paying more to sail in them than the schooners had earned in a dozen years of freighting.

16. The *Frank Brainerd* — Connecticut River brownstone freighter to Cape Verde packet. Copy of a Willard Jackson photo owned by Captain F. E. Bowker.

Across from the Maine Central pier, still further to the north, was the Cobb & Butler shipyard where many handsome vessels had taken the water. Here, the handsome *Frank Brainerd* had been built for her original Connecticut owners. She had been designed by the famous J. J. Wardwell, who was responsible for the smart looks and excellent performances of many of the Cobb & Butler vessels. The last schooner to leave their ways was the four-master *Josephine McQuesten,* launched in 1920. Owned largely by the McQuesten Lumber Co. of Boston, she was intended for the southern lumber trade.

The rest of the waterfront down to Tillson's wharf, where the Boston boats came in, was a jumble of old wharves, some in good repair and others unused except as graveyards for old coasters condemned as unseaworthy and left to rot. At one of these, a once-handsome little bay coaster, the *Agnes Mabel,* settled tiredly to the bottom after some fifty years of service, following her deceased owner to the final port from which no ship or seaman ever returns. She was still there two or three years later when the ancient but saucy *Rozella,* still working, tied up at the next wharf to discharge a load of wood. Built as a fishing schooner in 1840, the tough little vessel was put into the coasting trade when she was adjudged useless as a fisherman. She was as bluff-bowed as one of Columbus' caravels, and her wide, square stern showed traces of the archboard that had once adorned it. Unfortunately, stranding accomplished what sheer age had failed to do, and she went to pieces in 1921 after getting ashore at Port Clyde.

There were any number of these little old-time fishermen that turned to the coasting trade in their later years. Until well into

17. One version of a "shin-cracker" (traveling) wheel. The wheel moved from side to side with the tiller on which it was mounted. A helmsman got plenty of exercise, but that was about the only virtue which could be assigned to the rig.

Labels within image: After House, Compass Port, JOHN LEAVITT

18. The fixed wheel with tackles rigged.

the twenties, a visitor to Frisbie's wharf at Kittery might see the hulk of the old *Myra Sears,* built at Essex, Massachusetts, in the days of hemp rigging and "shin-cracker" wheels. Her shrouds were of hemp as big as a man's arm and made the wire rigging of later vessels look almost dainty by comparison. The shin-cracker was more properly known as a "traveling wheel" since it was mounted directly on a big square tiller, just clear of the deck, which moved from side to side as the wheel was turned. It was counted by most coastermen as an invention of the devil. It replaced the hand tillers with which small vessels were steered in the old days, but how much of an improvement it was is dubious. It was a miserable steering gear when one was striving to keep a wildly yawing schooner from broaching to as she ran off before the wind. It was replaced generally in later years by an arrangement in which the wheel was fixed but still controlled the movement of the short tiller by tackles. At least one coaster, however, built as late as 1890, was equipped with a shin-cracker. It may have pleased her original skipper but the later ones cursed it with fervor.

Other ex-fishermen of the same vintage as the *Myra Sears* were the *Revenue,* built at Essex in 1837, and the *Sarah Franklin,* only a few years younger. Both were owned in the Union River Bay region and were in operation until about the time of the First World War.

Other old-timers which deserted the fishing banks for the coasting trade included a number of "pinkys." These were double-ended craft, usually bluff in the bow with finer lines aft and distinguished in appearance by the way the bulwarks were carried out aft of the sternpost to a narrow stern board, notched at the top to act as a crotch for the main boom, the bulwarks sweeping high in the air to give them a saucy appearance like a bird with its tail in the air. They were invariably schooner-rigged and ranged in size from 40 to 60 feet in length. There were a few larger or smaller, but most of them were of the approximate dimensions noted. The little *Mary,* of only 7 net tons, built in 1811 at Portsmouth, New Hampshire, was working out of Friendship, Maine, until well into the twentieth century. She was at last bought by Admiral Peary to be preserved at his Casco Bay summer home.

Among the larger pinkys, the *Metamora* became well known as a coaster in her later years. She registered 35 tons and had been built at Gloucester, Massachusetts, in 1834. As a coaster, she carried granite, wood, coal, and any other bulk cargoes available. She hailed from Waldoboro for a number of years but was owned in New Harbor when she came to the end of her career. With a strong offshore wind blowing one night, she apparently parted her anchor chain and blew out of the mouth of the landlocked refuge and landed on New Harbor Sunken Ledges, where she pounded her bottom out.

The tiny pinky *Susan,* of only 16 tons, built in Essex in 1820, was used in the coasting trade in her later years and also "sailed parties" of "rusticators," when owned by Captain Charles Farrin of South Bristol in the nineties. He sold her to Mt. Desert Island where she continued to operate for some years as a "kiln-wooder," being about ninety years old when she disappeared from the ship registers.

One of the most typical pinkys, the last survivor of the type

19. The pinky *Maine* pictured in Belfast, Maine, during her later working days. Courtesy Peabody Museum, Salem, Massachusetts.

20. The pinky *Susan* in her last berth. Courtesy
John Quincy Adams.

in down-east waters, was the 34-ton *Maine,* named appropriately enough for the state where she spent the greater part of her life. She had been built at Essex to go hand lining on the Grand Banks, and for many years fought the fogs and gales of the Atlantic, but was at last forced to find other means to a livelihood. For a time, she continued to fish on the grounds nearer home but eventually was sold to become a packet schooner, owned in Sedgwick, and later, in ports further east. In her last days she was owned in Jonesport and was not broken up until the mid-1920s. At one time there was some talk of trying to preserve her as the last example of a true pinky but nothing came of it. After lying idle for several months, she was broken up and her stout old hull reduced to firewood.

The origin of this type of craft is uncertain. It first made its appearance as a Chebacco boat in the eighteenth century, Chebacco being the old name of Essex. Originally these craft were rigged as cat schooners with no bowsprit and little upsweep to the bulwarks aft. As the years went by, bowsprits were introduced, and the narrow, dory-like sternboard, called the "tombstone," rose higher and higher. No one seems to know for sure just when the name "pinky" was adopted or its origin. Some have felt it may have been taken from a type of Mediterranean craft called a Marseilles "pinque," which had some of the characteristics that later distinguished the pinky. In any event, they were handy little vessels, fast and able for their time and were much favored by early nineteenth-century fishermen. In 1851 an American fishing fleet was trapped during a gale in the Gulf of St. Lawrence and at least

two pinkys were among the few vessels which managed to beat out to sea.

Many other types of craft not native to the locality could be seen around Rockland in the later years. Aside from Chesapeake Bay, Maine was one of the last coastal areas to give up sail, and for many years after the turn of the century, small vessels were bought from "up to the west'ard" rather than being built.

A familiar sight at Glover's lumber wharf in Crockett's Cove was the *William H. Jewell,* once a Hudson River "bricker," but for many years employed in bringing lumber to Glover's from remote areas along the eastern coast. Glover owned most of her shares although Captain Levi Mitchell owned better than a master's interest.

Those who knew the *Jewell* only in her last years, when she was hardly more than a floating wreck, will find it difficult to believe that she was once a handsome little schooner with a tall rig and something of a reputation as a "heeler." She was painted green with a broad white stripe and had most of her original sheer. A cutwater and billet head decorated the bow and she had a main topmast in addition to her tall lower masts. Like most of the vessels built to freight brick on the Hudson, she was wide and shoal draft — a centerboarder — and she could reach and run with the best of them. Some of the bay coasters could leave her astern if working to windward, but let the wind come aft so the sheets could be started and she was off in a smother of white water.

I had a minor experience with Captain Mitchell that is amusing to look back on, although at the time I was covered with con-

21. The *George W. Collins* in her later years. Author's collection.

fusion. I had come to Rockland in another schooner whose skipper had been at odds with the *Jewell's* master over some kind of a deal, and when we passed the *Jewell* on the way into the harbor, my old man in answer to my question said something about the schooner being all right but that her master was "meaner than hell." A few days later, while prowling around the Rockland waterfront, I came upon the *Jewell* discharging a cargo of lumber at Glover's wharf. Several men were working on the lumber cargo, and after I had been obviously admiring the schooner for several minutes, one of them dressed in ordinary cap and overalls said, "What d'you say Sonny, want to go in her?" Recalling what my skipper had said, and being too young and foolish to exercise prudence, I attempted to look wise and replied, "Nothin' doin'. I hear the skipper's meaner than hell." There was a roar of laughter from the others and a grin from the man who had asked the question. It was Mitchell himself and, fortunately for me, he had a sense of humor. I felt about a foot high and my swagger as I walked away couldn't have been very convincing. At least, however, I learned the fallacy of taking everything literally — and, above all, of repeating it.

In this same cove at a wharf belonging to her owner, Charles Bicknell, died the old *Mary Brewer* at the age of seventy-one. She was a 90-ton, two-master built at Castine in the early fifties for the lumber trade, principally out of the Bangor River.

Here also passed one of my old schooners, the *George W. Collins,* built at East Lamoine in 1876. The skipper got into difficulties with the law sometime after I had left her and when he went to prison, the vessel was left to go to pieces in the mud. I found the remains almost thirty years later, and managed to salvage a deadeye from the rusted gang of rigging that lay in a tangle among the rotting timbers.

When W. S. Hodgkins launched the *Collins* from his yard in the centennial year, she was described in the shipping papers as being a "handsome clipper schooner, built for the stone trade and named for Captain George W. Collins of Bluehill, Maine."

When I was in her some forty-three years later, she was in bad shape — literally. Her once handsome stern had been rebuilt with green lumber, hacked out roughly with an ax. The transom planking curled at the edges and a new section of taffrail and stern timbering had been installed in the crudest possible fashion. She was so badly hogged that the stern drooped into the water, even when almost light. Her spars were blackened and her sails and gear were castoffs, purchased from marine junk dealers or salvaged from old wrecks. She leaked like the proverbial basket and was infested with bedbugs and cockroaches. She did have a beautiful bow (if one could disregard scabby paint and gaping seams), and I think it was no more than that which lured me aboard. She had a beautifully curved cutwater which terminated in a handsome billet head with sweeping trailboards and carved scroll work. There was something about her that reminded one of a once beautiful woman become a raddled old harridan but retaining a hint here and there of past beauty.

6 | LIMERS

Up at the "north end" of Rockland were the wharves of the Rockland-Rockport Lime Co. For many years, the lime industry was paramount in the Rockland area. Up back of the city were huge quarries and a narrow guage railroad came down into the city and extended along the entire waterfront. In the earliest days, Thomaston had been the center of the industry, and at that time Rockland was a part of that township. Later it was separated from Thomaston and began to come into its own as the center of the lime trade. Rockport, although small, also produced lime in great quantities, practically all of it being shipped out in vessels. In the last years methods of manufacture changed and so did methods of transportation.

Steel barges replaced the schooners almost completely and this caused some bitterness locally. As so often happens in a community where one big company or combine employs so many, changes are not always welcomed. With the new methods, vessels and people were thrown out of employment, and judging from some of the newspaper stories, feeling ran high in some quarters.

At the turn of the century the lime company owned 150 schooners of which half ran regularly to New York or Boston, loaded with casks of lime. The rest were employed in bringing wood to feed the voracious kiln fires. By 1910 the number of their schooners had dwindled to ten and at the time of the First World War only the *Mary Langdon, Morris & Cliff, Catawamteak,* and *John J. Perry* survived.

A few "outside" vessels carried lime, notable among them the ancient *Charlie & Willie* of 123 tons, built at Damariscotta in 1849 for the coastal and West Indian trades. She originally had three or four yards on her fore topmast but these gave way in later years to the more easily handled gaff topsails. Although not very large, she had the appearance of a deep waterman, deep in the waist, her main rail being between 3 and 4 feet above the deck. Her deckline was so full that her catheads projected out almost ahead and around the bow; she looked like some of the old Liverpool packet ships. The poop ran forward of the mainmast and her stern was large and square as an Indiaman's. Through superhuman efforts at the pumps, Captain Frank Robbins and his crew managed to deliver her lime cargoes unslaked until October, 1923, when she caught fire while lying in the Harlem River in New York and sank at her dock. She was then so old and so badly damaged by the fire that she was not considered to be worth the cost of repairs so she was abandoned.

Fire was, of course, the occupational hazard of the lime trade. Coasters always leaked to some extent, and every so often one of them would take in enough water to reach the casks of lime, even though they might be dunnaged well above the ceiling of the hold. Invariably a fire would be started that became a conflagration unless prompt and drastic action were taken. It was useless to pour more water on the fire, and the only recourse a skipper had was to attempt to smother the blaze through lack of air.

In the nineties the schooner *Herman F. Kimball* provided a notable example of this sort of action. She was off the coast bound to the westward with a cargo of lime when it was discovered to be on fire. Kittery was the nearest port and the skipper squared away for it at once, and before long was anchored behind the ledges which form a natural breakwater off Fort McClary. All hands got their clothing and possessions out on deck and a cask of lime was broached to make plaster with which to seal up all the cracks and crevices which might admit air below decks. One of the sails was unbent to make a tent over the boom and the men settled down to await the time when they might expect the fire to be extinguished. In the ensuing weeks a cautious peek below only indicated the fire was still smouldering and the hatch was hastily replaced and replastered. Patience was rewarded at last some three months later, when the blaze was found to be completely extin-

22. The venerable *Charlie & Willie,* formerly a topsail schooner in the West Indian trade, lastly a "limer." Courtesy Peabody Museum, Salem, Massachusetts.

23. The lime-laden *Herman F. Kimball*. Frank Wilson photograph, courtesy Captain W. J. L. Parker.

guished. Needless to say the damage was great, but after the hold was cleaned out and temporary repairs made, she was sailed back home to be rebuilt. Once again she appeared on the coast, rejuvenated and looking as well as she had for many years. She had been built at East Boothbay in 1888 by George M. Hodgdon, and she came to her end in 1918 when she drifted ashore at Peebles' Cove on Cape Elizabeth after missing stays while trying to beat into Portland. Her lumber cargo was salvaged but the vessel never came off.

Most of the schooners like the *Mary Langdon, Morris & Cliff* and *Catawamteak,* built or rebuilt particularly for the lime trade were given what was called a "riz" (raised) deck. The poop was extended forward to the fore rigging, level with the main rail, the original main deck and beams having been removed. The bulwark planking was made heavier and the whole structure became as tight as the rest of the hull. An open fly rail with turned stanchions was installed all around to complete the job. This made room for an additional tier of lime casks below deck where there was less danger of water getting to it.

The *Mary Langdon* was the matriarch of the late survivors, having been built at Thomaston in 1845 although she had been extensively rebuilt in the intervening years. When she was finally sold, she went into general freighting for a time, and her owner then tried a stint at rum running. She was apprehended by the Coast Guard, seized, condemned, and sold at auction. Osgood Gilbert bid her in, loaded her with lumber, and headed her for Florida where the land boom had started and building materials were in demand. Captain Frank Barter took her out but she never

made it to her destination; she stranded on the way and became a total loss.

The *Catawamteak* was built at I. L. Snow's yard in 1864 and was commanded for several years by Captain Will Kalloch. One of his sons, Charles, started a sea life with his father aboard the old vessel but later went into steam, where he became an officer, then master, and at last a top executive ashore for one of this country's largest steamship lines. After the lime trade died, the vessel was owned principally by Charles Bicknell of Rockland and was engaged in general trading. It was while bound up to the westward with a cargo of stone that her tired old hull opened up and she slipped down to her final home in Davy Jones' locker. She had survived several strandings and other mishaps through her long career, but her day had passed, and she was saved from the ignominious death of rotting away on some creek or deserted wharf in the lean years to come.

The *Morris & Cliff* had originally been named *Sam Weller* but, like many other vessels, was so completely rebuilt that an entire new documentation was issued, giving her date of build as 1890 and the place as Rockland, Maine. Originally, she was a well-decked schooner with a short poop built at Lyme, Connecticut, in 1868. After rebuilding, she was named for Morris and Clifford Perry, sons of one of the principal owners.

I was in her one winter running fertilizer to St. Stephens, New Brunswick, and returning to Boston with lumber. Captain R. C. Anthony, her master, was one of the few coasting skippers who liked to run things deep water fashion. It was reported that he used to go mate in some of the Cape Horners, and while he was

24. The *Mary Langdon*, lime coaster, rum runner, and lumber drogher during an eighty-year career. Author's collection.

no "bucko," he was far different from most of the easygoing coastermen. I had shipped as cook and the first time we got under way, I rushed on deck to bear a hand. The old man met me with a curt command to get back to my galley. If he wanted me on deck, he'd damn well call me!

Although we slept in the after house, the galley was still located forward in the sunken deckhouse that had sheltered both galley and forecastle in her early days as a "hand-puller." In her later years, the hoisting engine occupied the former forecastle.

I soon found out that my only duties on deck were to take the wheel during mealtimes and to help tend headsheets on the rare occasions when we were beating to windward. In square riggers, the time-honored task for the cook is tending the foresheet, and tending headsheets in a schooner is the nearest equivalent to it. There was no smoking at the wheel, and if the mate or I had occasion to come aft, we always did so by way of the lee quarter alley. We even tacked a "sir" on our "yesses" and "nos." In most of the small coasters the skipper was usually addressed simply as "Cap'n" or "Cap'n Jim," and in a few rare instances by his first name only. There was seldom any slackness in obeying an order but formality was at a minimum in that quarter of the maritime world.

It was an easy berth in the *Morris & Cliff* but a rather boring one, and I quit when the warmth of the galley was not as alluring as it had been during the colder weather. The old schooner also came to her end while heading south for Florida with a cargo of lumber for the Florida building boom, stranding at Bogue Inlet, North Carolina, in January, 1926.

One noted old schooner that became a limer was the *Telegraph*, of 122 tons, built in Boston in 1847 for the West Indian fruit trade. She is credited with having brought the first load of bananas to Boston while under the command of Captain Lorenzo Baker, a well-known Cape Cod skipper, thus marking the beginning of the famous United Fruit Company. Until quite recently a huge painted sign to that effect was still to be seen on the side of a building at Long Wharf, Boston, formerly occupied by the company.

In her later years, the *Telegraph* was sold to Thomaston owners, had her deck "riz up," and entered the lime trade, running to Boston and New York. When the trade languished, she was hauled up on the bank of the Georges River at Thomaston near the old Creighton lime wharf, and there she died. Her keel and lower frame futtocks can still be seen in the mud and some of the wrought iron bolts and spikes are as hard and unrusted as the day they were driven into the wood.

25. The *Lucy May,* a typical lumber schooner of her time, named for
the mother of her first master, Captain George Eldridge.
Courtesy Roger C. Peterson.

7 | PUMP OR SINK

Deep water sailors would have soon left vessels that leaked the way most coasting schooners did, but down east a leaking schooner was so commonplace in the later years that the attitude seemed to be it was cheaper to pump than to have the vessel properly repaired. In the *George W. Collins* we had to pump her twice a day in ordinary weather, with the skipper's son and I manning the hand pumps, and the deck engine operating a third pump forward. At that, it took at least half an hour of steady pumping before we could get a suck. In bad weather we pumped all the time.

The first trip I made in her, we loaded salt fish at T wharf in Boston for the East Coast Fisheries processing plant in Rockland. It was a little like carrying coals to Newcastle but the company was buying fish everywhere and judging by the load we put under hatches, they weren't very selective about it. Although salted, the fish didn't look or smell too healthy when they came aboard, and by the time we had laid out a calm, hot spell, they hadn't improved any.

A heavy southeaster caught us to the eastward of Thacher's Island when we finally did sail and, before long, we had a reef in the mainsail and the pumps were spouting green water. I am sure we pumped at least half the Gulf of Maine through that cargo of salt fish and by the time we fetched Rockland breakwater the water was well over the keelson and gaining all the time, despite our efforts at the pumps. Between previous deterioration and bilge water, the condition of our cargo was indescribable, and when they took our hatches off at the discharging pier, they hastily replaced them and hauled us across to the fertilizer factory where they bailed the maggoty cargo out in tubs. We finally managed to get her free of both cargo and bilge water, and after affecting crude repairs and filling gaping seams, the old man put her in the short-haul boxboard trade from Somesville to Rockland. Between the smell and the newly discovered presence of "wild life" in the form of swarms of bedbugs, I had enough after one trip and left hastily to go in the *Lulu W. Eppes* with Captain Freeman Closson and his wife Bertha. She was an immaculate housekeeper, and when I went aboard, a tub of lye water was waiting in the hold. Into it I dumped everything I owned and before many minutes, the water was dark with defunct bedbugs. A second tub of clean fresh water was waiting for me personally with a big cake of yellow soap and a scrub brush. When I finally emerged on deck, I felt (and probably looked) like a new man — or boy. That was my only experience with the pests, for I never went in a vessel thereafter if there was the slightest suspicion she was buggy.

Not all vessels leaked as badly as the *Collins,* but in any fleet of coasters in the later years, the predominant early morning sounds were those of clanking pumps and the swish of bilge water spouting from the scuppers. Some of the larger schooners had special pumping engines installed and they were seldom stilled. These old packets were almost literally pumped from port to port, and even then they sometimes didn't make it.

The 104-ton *Lucy May,* built for the lumber trade at Cherryfield in 1888, turned to the stone trade in her later years, and her owners thoughtfully provided her with good pumping gear. It was well they did, for on one trip bound to Boston she showed signs of opening up badly outside Portland. Captain Granville Robbins headed her in with every pump spouting green water and she barely fetched up alongside a wharf when she settled to the bottom, bolt upright, with her crew standing in water up to their waists on top of the deckhouse. In such shallow water it was a comparatively easy job to get the stone out of her so she was soon raised and repaired. Sometime later she was sold to W. H. Todd of Baltimore where she resumed her original trade of hauling lumber — this time from Virginia to the upper Chesapeake Bay ports.

Not so lucky was the big *Oakes Ames* of 254 tons, the largest two-master on the coast at the time. Built at Noank, Connecticut, in 1862 for the coal trade, she endured this hardest of all coaster freighting for many years before she became a lumber drogher. She was big for a two-master and in her last years needed all the men she could get, not only to sail her but to pump. As can be imagined, few hands were attracted to her and in lieu of men, engine pumps were installed fore and aft. She made a few trips to Lynn, Massachusetts, in the boxboard trade and on one of the last ones she was leaking so badly it was possible to hear the water running into her hold like a bathtub filling up. She was finally hauled into a backwater and abandoned.

This happened to many of the schooners in the declining years of the coasting trade. Even though there was fairly good business and freights were reasonably high, it seldom paid to make extensive repairs on the larger and older vessels. They had been neglected too long and the bigger they were the more it cost to repair them.

Even in the earlier days when vessels were in better condition, pumping was a large part of the day's activities at sea. The crews hated it and on occasion refused to pump. In such instances most skippers headed for the nearest port where repairs could be made on either a permanent or temporary basis. One captain, however, refused to be coerced, according to the story known all along the coast for years. The vessel was well offshore, bound south with a cargo of stone. The crew were pumping every watch and finally declared they would pump no more unless the vessel were headed in for the nearest harbor. The skipper listened to their demands thoughtfully and then turned away to go below. "All right, boys," he said as he went, "go ahead and throw the pump

26. The big *Oakes Ames,* 254 tons; largest (and leakiest) two-master on the coast in the twenties. Courtesy Maine Maritime Museum.

27. The *Charles H. Trickey* and *Mary E. Olys* sunk at Cape Porpoise. Author's collection.

brakes overboard if you want to. I've got as many friends in hell as you have!"

In the years following the First World War, hardly a week went by that some vessel wasn't reported to be on bottom full of water or had to be towed in, floating on her lumber cargo.

Early in 1919, the 300-ton three-master *Charlotte T. Sibley,* bound from New York for Rio de Janeiro, sprang a bad leak and foundered, her crew and several passengers being rescued at the last minute by the U.S. battleship *New Mexico.* The big three-master *Albert H. Willis,* leaking badly and on the verge of sinking, just made it to Norfolk with her cargo of logwood. In August, the two-master *Ella Clifton* from Weymouth, Nova Scotia, for Boston, was towed into the latter port floating on her lumber cargo, and a few days later the big *Pochasset* arrived half full of water, her crew pumping steadily as a towboat snaked her in for repairs. In November, the two-master *Hazel Dell* sank at her wharf in East Boston, her crew barely missing the trip to the bottom with her. The worst did happen when the *Mary E. Lynch* sank in New York. Loaded with stone, she was anchored off the Jersey shore when a tug ran into her early one December morning and she went down instantly, taking four of her crew with her. A list of all the vessels involved would include almost the entire coasting fleet. Nearly every vessel at one time or another wound up beneath the surface. Most of them were raised and repaired, of course, but many others were stripped and abandoned.

Losses were not all due to sinking, and quite a few were lost by stranding, fire, and collision. Captain Bennett Coleman lost the three-master *George D. Edmands* by fire about 300 miles off

28. Floating on her cargo. A vessel loaded with lumber could not sink and not infrequently wallowed into port practically submerged but still repairable.

the coast when bound from Norfolk to Bermuda with coal. The crew was picked up by a steamer bound for Rotterdam and perforce made a trip to Holland.

The 242-ton two-masted *Pochasset* piled up on Trundy's Reef while working her weary way into Portland in November, 1920. She had been weeks getting that far along the coast from Nova Scotia. Her crew of five men were all rescued by a boat from the Cape Elizabeth lifesaving station, but in a few days there was not even a vestige of the schooner, which had been built at Mystic, Connecticut, in 1872. Another big two-master, the *A. F. Kindberg,* stranded at Cape Porpoise, Maine, early in December of 1919; and on New Year's Eve, the three-masters *Charles H. Trickey* and *Mary E. Olys* were both wrecked in the channel trying to make the same harbor to escape a northeast blizzard which had struck down suddenly all along the coast.

Oddly enough, United States submarines accounted for four losses as a result of collisions. In November, 1919, Captain Black lost the schooner *Oakwoods* in Buzzards Bay when she was run down and sunk by the R-3. He later took the government award, went back to the Sound, and bought the *Mattie,* the ex-*Grace Bailey,* which is still operating in Penobscot Bay as a dude cruise vessel. In August of 1920, the schooner *Itasca,* a 71-ton two-master built at Cherryfield in 1879, was run down and sunk by an American submarine off Brenton Reef light vessel. The third loss in this fashion was the British schooner *Con Rien* bound for Charlottetown, Prince Edward Island, from New York and sunk outside Block Island by the U.S. submarine K-4. The three-master *Charlotte W. Miller* was the fourth casualty outside New London.

Later in the twenties, the *Rebecca R. Douglas* was sunk by the *S.S. Eastern Crown* in Pollock Rip Slue, and the three-masted *William Booth,* stone laden, was cut down and sunk by the four-master *Helen Barnet Gring.* The *Douglas* was raised, but the *Booth* was a total loss.

By 1930, the fleet of small coasters had shrunk to no more than fifty or sixty vessels, and before the outbreak of the Second World War, they, too, had vanished from the scene.

8 | LUMBER DROGHERS

THE majority of the Maine coasting fleet, particularly in the later years, depended upon lumber cargoes in one form or another to pay their dividends. From the eastern ports of Calais and Machias came dressed building lumber, called "square-edged" in the trade. Some was even loaded in Nova Scotia or New Brunswick, although the bulk of the lumber from over the border came in Canadian vessels.

Boxboards were shipped from the area around Mt. Desert Island and Penobscot Bay as well as from other places on the river banks as far west as the Sheepscot.

As I recall it, freights on lumber from Calais, Maine, New Brunswick, or Nova Scotia to New York were from $6 to $7 per thousand feet in the early twenties. Boxboard freights to Lynn or Boston were higher, but a schooner that could stow 100,000 feet of building lumber could not handle more than 85,000 feet of boxboards.

Other forms of lumber shipped up to the westward on occasion were piling, staves, laths, pulpwood, and cordwood. A once brisk trade in these cargoes had dwindled to almost nothing as the

years went by. Changes in construction methods and materials and rail and truck transportation deprived the coasters of a formerly lucrative business.

Money could be made in the lumber trade still if enough trips could be made and the vessels kept free from accident. Most schooners, however, did well if they averaged seven or eight trips a year, and many of them didn't complete more than four or five. In the earlier days, many of them went back east with paying cargoes but in the later decades, the eastbound cargoes grew fewer and fewer. Once in a while a load of coal or coke might be available at freights around $2 per ton. Many had to return with empty holds and at times they arrived down east to find they might have a long wait for another lumber cargo. The receipts made it possible to keep the vessels going, paying the grub bills and the crew's wages, but there was small margin for repairs — which even in those days of cheap labor and moderate shipyard charges could run into thousands of dollars.

Cargoes were usually handled by the crews aboard the vessels. They would take the lumber in over the rail and stow it and discharge it over the rail to stevedores or lumberyard workers at the port of discharge.

Most of the building lumber was spruce with occasionally some pine, hemlock, or fir. It might be in the form of 7/8-inch boards or any of the other standard sizes and types of building material. Because of its trimmed edges, it stowed well both in the hold and as a deckload. It was laid straight fore and aft, beginning in the hold. Once that was full, the hatches were clapped on and covered with tarpaulins, and the deckload started. Stakes were used where necessary along the rails to contain the lumber once the deckload had risen above the height of the main rail. Openings were left around the pumps and wherever necessary to get at gear on deck and to give access to aft companionways or forecastle doors. The gear, however, was usually brought up to the top of the deckload by shackling lower footblocks and others to wire or chain pendants where necessary. All vessels in the lumber trade usually had what was called a lumber pin rail lashed to the shrouds above the level the deckload would reach and all gear was made fast on these. "Lumber reefs" in sails were also common, for the deckloads were frequently high enough so a sail could not be fully hoisted above it, and it would have reduced the sail area too much to use the first regular row of reef points.

Once the deckload was topped off, lashings were run between the stakes from side to side, and lifelines were usually rove off between the shrouds, fore and aft.

Big two-masters and small three-masters of between 200 and 250 tons were favored for the eastern lumber business, and the largest fleet of them worked out of the St. Croix River. Up to the turn of the century Bangor had been the greatest lumber port, but in the early twenties it was rare to see any vessel except an occasional pulpwood schooner working up or down the Penobscot River.

Some of the schooners in later years were "white-washed yankees": American-built vessels kept under U.S. registry but with the controlling interest actually owned across the border in New Brunswick or Nova Scotia. Being under U.S. registry, they could operate in the American coastwise trade where freights were somewhat higher, a trade prohibited to vessels under foreign registry.

Some of the Calais schooners were built down east while others had been brought from New York or New Jersey where schooners of this size had been popular in the coal trade in earlier years. Driven away from their original haunts by the introduction of tugs and barges into the coal trade, many of them found their way to Maine where they took new leases on life in the lumber business.

Many of them were hand-pullers, having no hoisting engines and, in some cases, not even power in the yawl-boats. Most of them leaked badly but few seamen worried, for with a hold full of lumber a vessel couldn't sink, and by dint of much pumping, occasional caulking, and superficial repairs, they managed to keep going as long as there was business for them.

Among the best-known vessels in the Calais lumber trade were the *Eatons,* originally built for and owned by H. F. Eaton & Sons of Calais. The *Sarah Eaton* was the largest, a big two-topmaster built at Calais in 1874 expressly for the lumber trade.

Bluff-bowed, deep-waisted, and homely, she was nevertheless a good carrier and paid fairly good dividends when smarter vessels failed to do so. She was a hand-puller, and I believe she carried a mate, two hands, and a cook, beside the master. In the early twenties, the latter was Captain Ed Pettegrew.

There were two other *Eatons* in the Calais fleet in the later years: the *Nellie* of 118 tons and the smaller *Freddie* of 89 tons, both built the same year as their big sister, the *Sarah,* in 1874. The *Nellie Eaton* was sold to Massachusetts owners about 1923 but was lost the next year when she stranded at Chance Harbor, New Brunswick, and became a total loss, her entire crew being drowned. The *Freddie Eaton* was sold to Nova Scotia registry also in 1923, but she, too, lasted only a short time after crossing the border.

A regular in the Calais fleet was the 147-ton *L. L. Hamlin,* built at Calais in 1871. She was recognizable anywhere for she still retained her clumsy wooden boat davits at the stern, and with only a main topmast aloft, she looked like an overgrown bay coaster. In her last years, her skipper was Captain Elmer Greenlaw of Deer Isle. In 1921 she stranded in the Damariscotta River and became a total loss.

One of the larger two-masters hauling lumber out of the St. Croix River was the *Telumah,* of 230 tons, built at Damariscotta in 1866. For many years she had obtained her lumber cargoes at Bangor but when that trade languished, she moved further east. In 1922 under Captain Frank Walter she went down east to load a cargo of lumber at St. Martins, New Brunswick. Unfortunately she got ashore and it was not considered worthwhile to attempt to

29. Hogged, leaky with blistered paint and gray patched sails, old schooners such as the *Seth M. Todd* limped along the coast until they almost literally fell apart.

30. **The** big *Sarah Eaton* of Calais, a good carrier. Author's collection.

salvage her so she was stripped and abandoned. That winter the ice froze solidly around the hulk and one morning she came away from her resting place and went to sea in the ice floe on the ebb tide. That night, she returned on the flood and for a time it appeared that her unmanned voyaging was over; but once more she went out with the ice, and this time she broke up and scattered her timbers all along the shore.

The 210-ton *Samuel Hart,* built at Waldoboro, Maine, in 1871, was another later member of the Calais fleet but foundered outside Portland in November, 1922, following a collision with the towboat *Wyoming.*

One of the older vessels was the *Orizimbo,* of 147 tons, built as a half brig at Gouldsboro in 1854. She had been rerigged as a fore-and-aft schooner in later years although she retained many of the characteristics of vessels built for the offshore trade. She was sold to Nova Scotia owners about 1921 and carried on for several more years before she reached the inevitable end about 1924.

One decrepit lumber drogher which hung on until the twenties was the 194-ton three-master *Seth M. Todd.* She was not really so old, having been built in Calais in 1875, but she looked worse than almost any vessel in the fleet. She was badly hogged, her three masts thrusting upward at various angles, and her topmasts had long since disappeared. With gray patched sails and jibboom drooping toward the water, she was anything but handsome. A friend who made a round trip to New York in her swore that her rail scarphs opened and closed half an inch or more each time a wave passed beneath her limber hull. She finally grounded out at Parrsboro, Nova Scotia, and never came off the bottom, being stripped and abandoned where she lay.

Another older three-master hailing from Calais in the later years was the *Lizzie Lane,* of 231 tons. She had been built at Searsport in 1874 for Captain A. G. Closson, who was her principal owner and master for over twenty years. She was a general trader at first but entered the lumber trade, first out of the Bangor River and later, the St. Croix. On her last trip in 1921 she was destroyed by fire at West Dublin, Nova Scotia, where she had gone to load.

Certain vessels seem to acquire personality for no real discernible reason and become better known than others. Such was the three-masted *John Bracewell,* once a smart West Indian trader of 224 tons, built at Bath in 1878. She later entered the lumber trade, and moved further east in time with the progressive stages of her decrepitude until she reached her final resting place on the mud at Parrsboro. Even in old age, traces of original good looks were visible. She once had a beautifully decorated bow and stern, and her captain's cabin would have made a modern yachtsman envious. She had a big double berth with carved archboard above supported by fluted pilasters and a beautifully made sofa and sideboard. In her last years they were chipped, splintered, and begrimed but still gave an indication of the workmanship of the Bath ship joiners.

Some of the schooners bought from ports up to the westward became just as well known as those built locally. Milford, Delaware, contributed two large two-masters to the fleet: the *Rebecca G. Whilden* of 220 tons, built in 1853 as a half brig, according to reports, and the *Samuel Castner Jr.,* 239 tons, built in 1865. The *Whilden* was documented in Boston and sailed for some time under the John S. Emery & Co. house flag, but in her later years was managed by Irving J. White. Two of her masters were Captain Willard Johnson and Captain Ingram Seabean. She sank in the Neponset River in the early twenties and was abandoned there after being stripped of her gear. The *Castner* was bought by people in the Chesapeake Bay area in 1921 and thereafter operated in the Virginia lumber trade, but she was out of the registers in another year or so.

The big two-masted *Moonlight,* 198 tons, built at Belleville, New Jersey, in 1855, became a Calais lumber carrier under the ownership of H. F. Eaton & Sons, and her first master out of Calais was Captain Andrew Martin. In 1922, Captain Oliver Church, formerly in the *James L. Maloy,* took her over and stayed with her after she was sold to William White of Boston and hailed from that city. She was lost or abandoned about 1926 when owned by Captain G. W. Newcomb.

Another big New Jersey schooner was the *Henrietta Simmons* of 218 tons, built at Leesburg, New Jersey, in 1865. She, too, operated in the Calais lumber trade until December, 1924, when she foundered.

Among the three-masters which came from the westward to the region around the St. Croix river was the 280-ton *Charles C. Lister,* built at Milford, Delaware, in 1883. Although owned in New York she ran steadily down east — coal down and lumber back to New York. She was completely dismasted off the coast late in 1919, but was towed in and rebuilt and refitted to sail for many years more.

The *Abbie C. Stubbs* of 354 tons was built at New Haven, Connecticut, in 1882, but for many years she traded down east and was manned by Maine captains and crews. Captain Steve Peabody had her for several years and she was much more at home east of Petit Manan than she was on Long Island Sound.

The sole possible survivor of the once-large Calais lumber fleet was, until comparatively recently, the big two-master *Allen Gurney,* which for many years since the twenties had been known to tourists as a tearoom at Nantucket. This metamorphosis took place about 1921 and she became a major attraction to summer visitors who liked to sip their tea in quaint surroundings.

Another old-timer from the New Jersey area which spent her last years in the down-east lumber trade was the 190-ton *Lizzie D. Small,* built in 1866 at Camden, New Jersey, for the coal trade. She hailed from Bangor when she was lost near Westport, Massachusetts, in 1922.

Most of the schooners hailing from Machias in the later years were smaller than the average Bangor or Calais vessels. A good example was the *Alaska* of 175 tons, built at East Machias in 1867. I have heard it said that she never carried a cargo to the westward that wasn't lumber in some form and that she never showed any other hailing port than "Machias" on her stern. She was owned in later years by E. I. White and lastly by Captain W. H. Strout. She came to her end in 1926 when she was abandoned in Nova Scotia where she had gone to load.

31. *Henrietta Simmons,* the fifty-five-year-old Jerseyman which ended her days as a Calais lumber drogher. Courtesy Peabody Museum, Salem, Massachusetts.

32. The *Alaska* — from launch in 1867 to abandonment in 1926, a Machias lumber carrier. Courtesy Peabody Museum, Salem, Massachusetts.

Other well-known Machias two-masters to be seen along the coast at the time of the First World War and immediately afterward were the *Annie Gus, Annie M. Preble, Bertha V., Herbert Loring,* and *Lizzie D. Peabody.*

The *Annie Gus* was sold to the far-off Dominican Republic but whether she ever reached her new home port is uncertain. She was a fairly old vessel of 99 tons, built at Pembroke, Maine, in 1871, and her long years in the lumber trade had made her pretty limber for an offshore trip.

The *Annie M. Preble* came to Boothbay Harbor in the later years under the ownership of Captain Al McIntyre. He operated her in no regular trade, often carrying fruit and farm produce to New York as well as any other cargo that would pay him to take. He finally sold her for use as a barge for the storage of explosives, and retired ashore. He lived to a ripe old age in his home town and owned his own wharf where he rented boats, sold marine equipment, and set moorings for yachtsmen. He died after World War II, well into his eighties.

The little *Bertha V.* of only 58 tons was one of the smallest lumber schooners in the later years. She was built in 1869 at Millbridge, Maine, and was owned for many years by the Machias Lumber Co., carrying building lumber on the long hauls to the westward. Captain S. E. Joy had her for several years and was succeeded by Captain Stephen Kingham. Captain George Eldredge had her for a time before taking over the *Anna Sophia.* For much of her life she carried two topmasts and a big sailing rig. In the thirties she was sold to Jonesport ownership. Her rig was cut down and she became a bay coaster, engaged principally in carrying pulpwood. Not long afterward she was hauled up on the bank at Little Deer Isle and abandoned.

The *Herman F. Kimball* became a regular in the lumber fleet after her days as a lime coaster and was loaded with lumber when she was lost at Cape Elizabeth in 1918.

The old two-masted *Franconia* built at Surry, Maine, in 1862 was another old-timer that hung on in the lumber trade for years, and in the late twenties she turned up in Boston looking surprisingly well for her age.

There were, of course, many schooners that carried lumber now and then and could not be said to be members of the lumber fleet.

In Ellsworth there were a number of vessels operated in general trade including, besides the *Lavolta, Storm Petrel,* and *Henrietta A. Whitney,* the *Nellie Grant* and *Ralph K. Grant.* The two latter were two-masters, built by Isaac Grant at his Ellsworth yard in the same year, 1873. The *Nellie Grant,* of 139 tons, went missing with all hands in 1925 when Captain Noah Kane of Surry was master. The *Ralph Grant* was sold further down east where she became a power cannery lighter.

One of the smartest schooners in the coasting fleet was the *Marguerite,* a 113-ton former clipper fisherman built at Essex, Massachusetts, in 1883. These vessels were flatter floored and harder bilged than their later sisters and often made excellent coasters. Most of them were somewhat reduced in rig when they came into the coasting fleet but not so the *Marguerite.* She was owned in Jonesport, J. V. Sawyer being the managing owner and Captain Paris Calor, the master. She could sail through the lee of

33. The tall-sparred little *Bertha V*. Courtesy John Quincy Adams.

34. The *Nellie Grant* of Ellsworth. Missing with all hands since 1925. Courtesy Peabody Museum.

almost any other coaster anywhere near her size and her stern was a familiar sight to all when we sailed in a fleet. Captain Emery Kelley was master when she was run down and sunk in Boston Harbor in the later twenties.

The big two-master *Mary Weaver* of 222 tons was built in Philadelphia in 1867 for the coal trade, but came east in her later years to hail from Portland. Coming down river from Wiscasset in October, 1918, she struck a ledge, stove in a couple of planks, and filled, floating on her lumber cargo. She was towed into Boothbay Harbor, the lumber was transhipped, and her aged hull hauled into Mill Cove and abandoned. For many years she was one of the familiar sights, looking small and desolate among the big four- and five-masted hulks that crowded the cove. Gradually she disintegrated, but her keel and some of her others timbers can still be seen above the mud.

Although sold south at the time of the First World War, one schooner well remembered along the coast was the 91-ton *Portland Packet,* notorious for having the longest main boom for her size on the coast. Reputed to be very fast, she was a brute to steer, probably because of her big rig, and this also may have been the cause of her loss in 1919, when she went missing while on a passage from New York to Mobile.

One old-timer that carried "Bangor" as a hailing port on her wide, square transom through the first war was the *W. D. Mangam,* an 89-ton two-master built at Taunton, Massachusetts, as far back as 1852. After many years in the coal trade she came down east to join the lumber fleet and at last was sold to Nova Scotia.

She appeared in Maine waters occasionally with loads of wood until the middle twenties.

Nova Scotia also became the home of the Belfast-built *Puritan* of 116 tons built in 1886. She had been owned by Captain C. H. Lynam of Seal Harbor, but when he got a good offer for her from a West Indian group he accepted it. The new owners sent her off to Nova Scotia to have some repairs made, but a few days later she put into Boothbay Harbor leaking and with sails blown away. Extensive repairs were made there, over $3,000 dollars reportedly being spent in July, 1920. Captain Lynam later owned the ex-stone sloop *M. M. Hamilton.* The *Puritan* never did get to the West Indies, but died on the mud at Parrsboro, Nova Scotia.

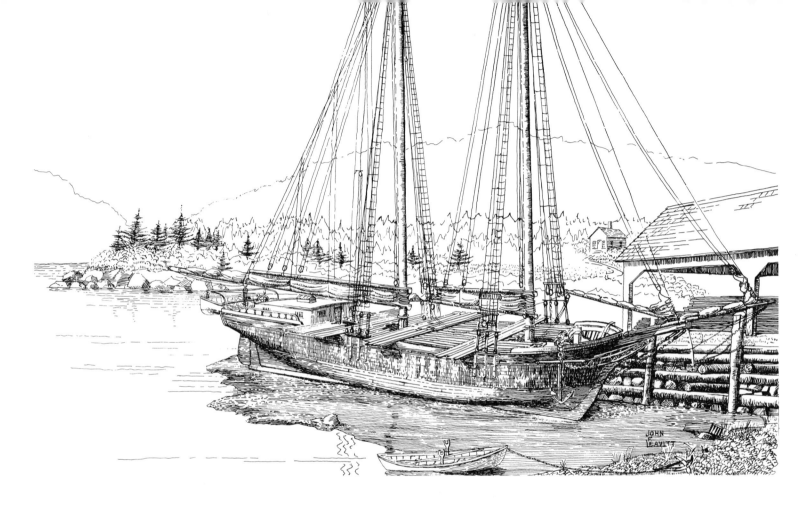

35. The old *George W. Collins* loading boxboards. The boards were stowed fore and aft in the hold and on deck up to the height of the rail. The next tiers, however, were alternated, first athwartships, then fore and aft, the fore-and-aft tiers being started amidships. There was no lashing on the deck-load, merely spikes driven down through two or three of the top tiers at random.

9 | BOXBOARDERS

LUMBER has always been a favorite cargo with coaster crews for it is clean, sweet-smelling, and ordinarily easy to handle. Boxboards, however, were viewed with resignation at best by the crews who had to handle them. They were from 7/8's of an inch to 2 inches thick, sawed from a spruce, pine, or hemlock log so the bark was left on the edges. They had to be handled one board at a time, and before long, uncalloused hands were torn and raw from the rough bark and splinters. Gloves were useless and expensive for they wore through in a few hours, and it was simply a matter of endurance until hands became calloused sufficiently to afford protection. In the meantime liberal applications of grease (usually mast "slush") and wrappings of old rags helped to ease the pain between working hours.

Because of the uneven edges, boxboards didn't stow as closely as square-edged lumber. In the hold it had to be stowed fore and aft, the same as any other lumber cargo and the same with the deckload up to the height of the bulwarks. Above them, however, the next tier of boards was laid athwartships projecting out several feet beyond the sides of the schooner between the fore and main rigging. The next tier was then laid fore and aft, beginning at the center line, and from then on the tiers were stowed alternately fore and aft and athwartships until the deckload had risen to a height of 4 or 5 feet above the main rail, "winged out" 3 feet or more beyond the hull on each side.

No lashing was possible, and other than the alternate direction of the tiers, the only fastening ever given a boxboard cargo were a few spikes driven in at random down through the top courses of boards, the last tier having always been laid athwartships. Strangely enough, there were very few instances of schooners losing part or whole of their boxboard deckloads. Of course, the trips were comparatively short and the vessels were not driven hard.

Spaces were left around the pumps and the gear was rigged just as other schooners carrying square-edged lumber did, with the footblocks brought to the top of the deckload by the use of chain pendants and the gear made fast on special pin rails lashed to the shrouds above the level of the deckload.

Despite the fact that deckloads were seldom lost, they were the cause of some anxiety, particularly in winter. Spray froze in the crevices, and in bad weather a schooner could get iced up to a

36. "Towing up" — the *Betsy Ross* of the Ross Towboat Co. in Boston used to tow most of the smaller coasters to the various discharge wharves in the area. Her skipper wore a "tar paper" (derby) hat and black half sleeves, and tucked a silk handkerchief around his neck to protect his stiff collar. The background in the drawing only suggests the city and is not a portrayal of any particular place.

dangerous degree. Fortunately, they never could be loaded deep with boxboards and there was more reserve buoyancy than in vessels already loaded decks to water with heavier cargoes.

Many schooners carried their boxboard cargoes to places like Page's box factory at Cambridgeport, Massachusetts. To reach the discharging wharf it was necessary to haul or be towed through the North End bridges spanning the waterway that cuts through the Boston & Maine railroad yards where the Charles River empties into the head of Boston harbor.

If a towboat were hired, it picked up the schooner in the outer harbor and usually towed alongside until the first bridge was reached. The yawl-boat was then cleared from the stern davits and lashed fore and aft under the bowsprit. The tug took up station astern and, as the bridges opened one by one, pushed the schooner up through the narrow and rather crooked channel. Coming to the end of the bridges a single lock had to be negotiated to reach the higher level of the Charles River Basin. Through the lock the tow continued across to the little canal that extended perhaps a quarter of a mile inland to the westward near Kendall Square. Here another draw had to be negotiated before the schooner could complete the last few hundred yards to the box factory wharf. In the river basin there was no tidal rise or fall so the work of discharging cargo went on steadily until all the lumber was on the wharf.

Some coasters used to haul through the bridges, running lines out ahead with the yawl-boat and then hauling themselves along by hand or with the hoisting engine. This was a long and laborious process, however, and in the last years hauling by hand was not allowed. Some of the skippers were bitter about it, as I remem-

37. The *Fannie F. Hall* being stripped of her disguise as a *Mayflower* replica for the Pilgrim tercentenary in 1920. She never re-entered the coasting trade, however. Courtesy Peabody Museum, Salem, Massachusetts.

38. The homely *Ella Clifton* with sagging hull and patched sails.
Courtesy John Quincy Adams.

ber, and blamed the towboat companies for having schemed to have the ruling put into effect. I think the towage fee through the north end bridges was approximately 50 dollars, in and out. The fee going up was greater than coming out for the charge was greater when the schooner was loaded. The charge for the south end bridges up to Dover street was about the same.

In the heyday of the boxboard trade, Lynn was the principal discharge port in Massachusetts Bay, however. It was still one of the most active shoe manufacturing cities in the country, and Hoague, Sprague & Co. operated one of the largest box factories in the east, using millions of feet of lumber a year building packing cases in which the shoes were shipped out. At their wharf off Broad Street, now a part of the Champion Lamp Works property, I have been in company with nearly a dozen schooners, two- and three-masters, discharging boxboards or awaiting their turn to do so. At Lynn discharging was all "tide work." Unloading went on from half tide through the peak of the flood and down to half tide again. This was due to the fact that even there the rise and fall of the tide was so great that it was impractical to attempt work when the schooners were grounded on the mud and the edge of the wharf was far above them.

Here the handsome *Alice S. Wentworth* queened it over the fleet, although dwarfed by the big *Oakes Ames*. Before her conversion to a poor replica of the Pilgrim ship *Mayflower* in 1920, the *Fannie F. Hall* was a regular visitor. She was of 93 tons register, built in Stockton, Maine, in 1867, and had been owned for many years by Captain Fred Hutchins of Orland. After selling her, he bought the *Ella Clifton,* a New Brunswick-built two-mas-

ter of 108 tons which had got ashore on the American coast and had been sufficiently rebuilt to entitle her to U.S. documentation for the coastwise trade. She was noted for being one of the ugliest looking schooners on the coast and even her owner made no effort to defend her against the allegation. She was badly hogged, with stumpy masts and almost square sails, her stem being almost plumb and her heavy square stern drooping in the water. When Cap'n Fred decided to retire, he sold her to someone in Kennebunkport and sailed her down there, but she never went to sea again and died on the bank of the river where her timbers were visible for many years thereafter.

Almost as odd-looking was the *M. M. Hamilton,* another boxboarder of 111 tons built on Chebeague Island in Casco Bay as a stone sloop in 1869. As a sloop, she had been a good-looking vessel with a handsome sheer, well-balanced ends, and a rig which was the largest of its type on the coast, the gigantic mainsail measuring over a thousand square yards. Her mast and bowsprit were tremendous, and in her later years, when she was rerigged as a schooner, these were simply cut down in length but not in diameter. As a result, the mainmast of normal size that was installed when the rig was changed looked much too small. Her cutwater, billet head and trailboards had long since been replaced by a stubby knee, and an ugly, high winch house had been built around the foremast. Since she had a low cabin trunk aft, the forward house looked like the obvious afterthought that it was. Her centerboard had been removed so her performance under sail was no better than her appearance, especially to windward.

She had luxurious accommodations for a coaster, however.

39. The *M. M. Hamilton,* schooner-rigged and loaded with lumber
near Pemaquid about 1920. Courtesy Roger C. Peterson.

All hands slept aft, and there were three double staterooms besides the master's cabin. In her later years she was usually sailed with a three-man crew, and each man had a room to himself. Her owner-master, Captain Clarence Lynam of Seal Harbor on Mt. Desert Island, was a huge gruff bear of a man with a partially crippled leg which got him the nickname of "Hoppy" along the coast. He was grim and gruff most of the time but his bark was worse than his bite.

When the *Lulu W. Eppes* was sold, I was "on the beach" at Ellsworth with only a couple of dollars in my pocket, having drawn heavily against my 15-dollar-a-month wages. I was too broke to get home by train and none of the Ellsworth vessels were in, or expected in, so I couldn't ship out in them. My folks were living in Massachusetts at the time, and cold weather was in the offing. At last I heard the *M. M. Hamilton* was loading at Somesville for Boston, so packing my seabag I hiked the 20-odd miles over muddy roads, arriving at the sawmill wharf, blistered but hopeful. Captain Lynam and his mate-cook, Len Duffy, were working the cargo into her when I arrived and when I asked the old man for a chance to earn my passage to the westward, he merely grunted. Thinking this indicated a refusal, I backed away, wondering what to do next. I had something like 30 cents left to my name and, while I could sleep in a convenient barn or even in the mill's sawdust pile if I had to, it was fall and there was beginning to be a chill in the air that didn't bode well for my comfort.

Suddenly there was a roar from old "Hoppy." "Well," he bellowed, "what the hell are y' standin' 'round there for? Put y' gear below and git to work. Think I'm goin' t' give y' passage y' don't work for?"

This didn't sound as though it would be an easy berth but beggars can't be choosers so I shucked off my coat and pitched into the lumber pile. The next day I got another shock when, after a morning of hard work handling 2-inch green birch and maple, we sat down to dinner at noon. Any fifteen-year-old youngster is perpetually hungry and I was no exception, particularly since my normal appetite had been accentuated by labor on the cargo.

I was working briskly on a large second helping of salt fish, potatoes, and pork scraps when I became aware the old man was glaring at me from under his bushy eyebrows. For a moment he continued to watch me eat — then he burst out with, "My God, Jack, you're all legs and appetite!"

Despite all this, when we arrived in Boston he said he was sorry to see me go and tendered $5 which he insisted I had earned. He also said he'd like to have me stay with him and, to cut the story short, I finished the season in the vessel and went back the next spring when he wired me to come down to help take the schooner out. What was more, he sent me the money to pay my train and boat fare. Financially, my rise in the world of coasters had been rapid. I had started in my first vessel at $10 a month, got $15 in the second one, and now I was drawing $20.

After some twelve hours on trains, ferry, and stage, I arrived at Seal Harbor and, after catching up on some sleep, we went over to Northeast Harbor where the schooner had been laid up for a couple of months. She had been sailing around her chains until

40. The *Regina* discharging boxboards at Hoague, Sprague's wharf in Lynn, Massachusetts. Author's collection.

they were twisted up in knots and it took several days to clear them. Once more the sails were bent and the gear rove off. It was cold work much of the time, but in the beautiful landlocked harbor it was very pleasant despite the chill in the air.

Our first charter was for a load of boxboards from Somesville to Cambridgeport, and before the week was out we were sailing up Somes' Sound, the yawl-boat pushing us through the narrows and into the "pool." The next day we began working the cargo into her. Several days later the last board of the deckload was stowed and we made preparations to get under way in the morning. That night, however, the old man woke us with a yell and demanded that we turn out and stand by to get under way. The mate and I looked at each other in amazement, and took a closer look at the skipper. His eyes were feverishly bright; it was apparent that he was sick and out of his head. We tried to tell him it was midnight, but he insisted it was an eclipse of the sun and that we had to get out of there.

We finally managed to get him back into his bunk and, the first thing in the morning, a doctor was summoned. It was quite a while before one arrived, for there was no doctor in town. The diagnosis was a case of pneumonia. By that time the old man was too sick to be rambunctious so we hoisted him out through the companionway in a chair and got him ashore and to a hospital in Bar Harbor.

After lying at anchor for the better part of the month, during which time I lived aboard alone as shipkeeper, Captain Jim Bray, formerly of the bay coaster *Circle,* took charge and the cook-mate having also returned, we sailed at once for Boston.

The new skipper was a brother of Captain John Bray, well known as master of deep water square-riggers in the South American trade. He was a martinet and had the reputation of keeping his vessels in the best possible condition. Under his command the handsome barkentine *Kremlin,* owned by John S. Emery & Co. of Boston, was known as "Emery's yacht." Cap'n Jim, however, was a typical coasterman, a good coastal pilot and seaman but there it ended. He was a very quiet man and spent most of the time pacing the deck, puffing away on a corncob pipe that was usually upside down. I finished the trip and left the *Hamilton,* for the atmosphere was a little too lugubrious for my youthful taste.

Here to Lynn also came the *Regina,* destined to achieve fame as the workshop and private museum of Booth Tarkington, who bought her in her old age and had her blocked up permanently beside his boathouse at Kennebunkport.

Registering 114 tons, the *Regina* was built in 1891 at Machias particularly for the lumber trade, and for many years she hailed from that port. She was a typical lumber carrier with high bulwarks and large hatches. When new, she carried large crews, and the forward house had once been the forecastle and galley. She was built in a yard where many offshore vessels were constructed and had much of the trim and fancy mouldings not usually wasted on coasters. Her buffalo rail aft was capped, and the stanchions and fly rail above it were excellent examples of the ship joiner's art. Her elliptical stern was heavy but nicely shaped, and the long cutwater sported a carved billet head and elaborately decorated trailboards. Although unused in later years, the bowports were still in the hull. She was well sparred, having the long

41. The boxboard deckload of the *Regina* "winged out" over the sides of the vessel. Courtesy John Quincy Adams.

topmasts and flying jibboom common to the older schooners and had she not been badly hogged, she would have been one of the handsomest vessels along the coast.

In the twenties Captain Emery Wallace of Peaks Island was master and owner. I believe he was at one time a deep-water mate, and although he was not noted particularly as a driver, he managed to keep the *Regina* moving in pretty smart fashion. He was one of the last survivors in the boxboard trade, and when it came to an end, he sold the old schooner to Tarkington and retired ashore.

The writer had her towed to Kennebunkport, cleaned up, painted, and put in good superficial condition, and for many years she was a great attraction for tourists. He used the after quarters for a workroom, and the *Regina* looked smarter than she had at any time since she was new. She outlived her famous owner by more than a decade, but after his death she was allowed to deteriorate, and after World War II, she was broken up.

A list of the schooners which carried boxboards to Lynn and Boston in the early to middle twenties would include the great majority of the surviving coasters of medium size in the state of Maine. Some of them appeared only occasionally, having other business elsewhere, while others ran steadily as long as the trade endured.

The little *Gold Hunter* of 54 tons, built at York, Maine, in 1860, made most of her last trips to Lynn, but her captain-owner, Ike Adams, died in the later twenties and the *Gold Hunter* was stripped and hauled up back of Billy Sawyer's store at Boothbay Harbor, and a wharf was extended out over her remains.

The *Gilbert Stancliff* was one of the regulars, both under Captain John Stevens and later, George Robbins. I was in her for several trips with Cap'n George and a young Nova Scotian whose name I have forgotten. For some time she was easily recognizable, for we carried the main topmast away and it was not replaced at once. "One-topmasters" were commonplace enough but invariably it was the fore topmast that was missing.

The big *James L. Maloy*, an ex-Jerseyman, came to the boxboard fleet from Calais when she was last owned by Osgood Gilbert of Boston. He was a native of Rockland, Maine, who had been in business in Mystic, Connecticut, with his brother Mark, the two of them having operated the Gilbert Transportation Co. there. He later came to Boston and established a ship brokering and chartering agency. He had been very successful before and during the First World War but like many others he was caught at the end of the conflict with too much tonnage on his hands and the bottom out of the freight market, so far as larger vessels were concerned. He continued to operate, however, and was the principal chartering agent for many of the smaller down-east schooners in the twenties. He owned a number of them, wholly or in part, and the *Maloy* was one. When business for even the smaller coasters began to drop off, he sold her to some people who took her to Onset, hauled her up on the bank, and made a tearoom of her. It was not a very successful venture and, in 1929, Gilbert bought her back for the Massachusetts Bay Tercentenary Committee who intended to build her into a replica of the Puritan ship *Arbella*. The work was to be done at Salem, but during the tow down the *Maloy* began to leak in alarming fashion and the tug hastened into Marblehead with her where she sank — fortunately at the head of the harbor, out of the channel. There she lay for some time, abandoned. Meanwhile, Gilbert, on behalf of the Tercentenary commission, purchased the *Lavolta* at Ellsworth and went ahead with her conversion for the original purpose.

The *Maloy* was adjudged a menace to navigation by the powers that be and a call went out for bids to remove the hulk and either sink or destroy it. Os Gilbert, with true Yankee acumen, put in a bid and was awarded the contract. He hired a tug and one of McKie's older lighters from Boston and at low tide brought the lighter in alongside the stranded hulk. The masts had been cut away previously and the waterlogged hulk stripped of anything that had value. The old wire rigging was used to lash her alongside the lighter, a couple of shrouds being worked under the bow and stern while the rest were made fast to the chainplates and toggled inboard of the lighter. The derrick of the lighter was swung above the old schooner and the falls hooked into strops through the outboard chainplates.

When the tide rose, the *Maloy* came reluctantly off bottom, hanging precariously in the lashings. Slowly, the tow out of the harbor began with everyone holding their breath and praying nothing would part. Once out of the harbor mouth in the swells outside, the hulk began to work alarmingly and it was soon obvious that she wouldn't get too far. Outside Marblehead Rock the lashings began to part and when they did, the wire whipped back over the lighter in frightening fashion. Everyone aboard dove out of the way for the snap of the wire would have taken a man's head off like an oversized bull-whip. Each parted lashing put more

42. The *M. M. Hamilton* as a sloop working on a breakwater.

43. The square-sterned *Grace E. Stevens, ex-John Henry.* Courtesy John Quincy Adams.

strain on the others and it was obvious there was nothing to be done but let her go, so axes were put to the other lashings within reach and the *Maloy* started her final plunge bottomward. There was no way to unhook the lighter's falls from the outboard chainplates, and the engineer could only release his compressor and let the wire overrun. Letting her get a good start on her dive, he then jammed down his compressor and with a tremendous jerk, the lighter rolled down and then snapped back on an even keel. When the falls were reeled in, it was found that the chainplates had been pulled completely out of the rotten hulk. The *Maloy* sank a good mile or so from the intended place of burial but soundings disclosed there was sufficient water so she could not possibly be a menace to navigation, and from that day on nothing has ever been seen of her.

The *George W. Collins,* my first schooner, made only a few trips to Lynn just after the war for she was getting too bad to venture far outside of Penobscot Bay, and during the rest of her active career she carted boxboards from Somesville to Rockland. It had not taken me long to discover that the skipper was too heavily addicted to "jakey" (Jamaica ginger extract) and $3 women. To a fourteen-year-old youngster, this was something of a shock, and I sought and found refuge with Freeman and Bertha Closson aboard the old *Lulu W. Eppes.* The skipper of the *Collins* wound up in difficulties with the law and went to the state prison at Thomaston for a long term, while the old schooner rotted away in Crockett's Cove at Rockland, where she had been laid up.

The *Grace E. Stevens* also ran only intermittently in the boxboard fleet, for her owner-master, Captain "Med" Eaton of Bluehill, had a lucrative contract carrying coal to the various lighthouses along the coast. In between times, however, she took whatever cargoes were offered, and we were always glad to see Cap'n Med and the *Gracie.* She was an old 87-ton schooner, built as the *John Henry* at Brookhaven, New York, in 1853, but sold down east in the eighties. She had been extensively rebuilt, and in the process her stern had been shortened and planked straight across without any camber and with very little rake. She was, therefore, almost as square-sterned as a "Johnny woodboat," one of those crudely built New Brunswick schooners that used to come in fleets to the Penobscot Bay area with wood for the lime kilns. The *Gracie* could never have been mistaken for any other vessel, for in addition to her square stern, she was painted with a gray hull and black bulwarks, an unusual color combination among the coasters. Captain Eaton was a gregarious and jolly old fellow who liked to visit and he was always welcome aboard any of the other vessels.

The three "limers," *Mary Langdon, Catawamteak* and *Morris & Cliff,* appeared occasionally with loads of boxboards but they always preferred under-deck cargoes if they could get them.

One of the larger and more interesting vessels in the later years was the 243-ton *Cameo,* owned and skippered by Captain Charles Trenholm of Fall River, Massachusetts. Her history was rather unusual, beginning in 1878 when she was launched from Goss & Sawyer's yard in Bath, Maine, as a half brig for the West Indian trade. She was for a long time owned by the Bartram Brothers of New York and freighted sugar from Cuba. Sometime in the nineties, she was rerigged as a fore and aft schooner, and later was sold to Nova Scotia. From there she was bought by some Portuguese-American whalemen at New Bedford and spent several years as a "blubber-hunter" cruising the South Atlantic grounds. Captain Trenholm bought her back from them and put her back in the general coasting trade, freighting boxboards much of the time. Even after several years of this, a faint scent of whale oil still lingered to hint at her previous occupation. She continued to operate into the thirties and was at last abandoned, I believe, at Frankfort Marsh, near the mouth of the Penobscot River.

A number of old schooners were brought out of retirement to carry boxboards in the twenties but the size of the fleet seemed to remain fairly constant. If a newcomer appeared, it was usually only to take the place of some vessel lost or abandoned when she couldn't keep afloat any longer.

One such ill-starred craft was the 134-ton two-master *Odell,* built at Bowdoinham on the Kennebec in 1873. In her earlier years, she had carried hay and lumber from Bangor to the westward. She had probably sailed in the same fleet as the fabled *Liza Jane* which, according to the old epic, "left port one day with a hold full of boards and a deckload of hay." After a long lay-up, she was bought by Os Gilbert. Under Captain J. M. Harford, she loaded boxboards at Lincolnville for Lynn and resumed her coasting career. On her last trip, she was leaking badly and had to put into Rockland where she squatted for a couple of days on the mudflats at the north end of the harbor. After a while, she became sufficiently "mudded up" and the leak moderated considerably so she started out again. That time, she got a few miles down the Muscle Ridge channel before she had to be beached on the mud at

44. The *Eugenie* caught in a squall off the coast. Author's collection.

Spruce Head. Eventually, she got as far as Portland but it was obvious that she just wasn't going to stay afloat, so they transshipped the cargo, stripped the schooner, and left her on the bank at the mercy of the elements.

"Muddin' " was a process similar to "inhaling" sawdust to stop a vessel from leaking. The schooner was simply grounded on a mudflat and the incoming tide carried enough mud into the gaping seams temporarily to stop the worst of the leaking. There were other expedients, and horse manure was considered to be particularly efficacious, although it was more difficult to obtain in quantity than sawdust or mud.

One rank outsider came to join the fleet when the *Fred Tyler,* a narrow-beamed New York "canal-er" showed up to load with others of the boxboard fleet at Wiscasset. She had been bought by Os Gilbert and resold to Captain Charley Peterkin and others of Medford, Massachusetts. She was the type of schooner built to negotiate some of the narrow canals and inland waterways in the New York–New Jersey area, carrying coal and similar cargoes. It was obvious she would be cranky with a high deckload.

Peterkin didn't have much experience in the lumber trade at the time, but with some assistance and advice from the other skippers, he got the *Tyler* loaded and sailed for Boston in the fall of 1920. Somewhere to the westward of Cape Elizabeth she started a butt or worked her caulking loose, and in no time at all she was floating on her cargo, wallowing dangerously and acting as though she would roll over on her beam ends at any moment. The crew took to the yawl-boat and got ashore about the time the *Fred Ty-*

ler hit the beach at Biddeford Pool. There she broke up, scattering lumber and gear all over the pool.

Also resorting to the boxboard trade to keep going in her old age was the 94-ton *Eugenie,* built at Millbridge in 1883 and hailing from Machias and, in her last years, from Portland. Like the *Regina,* she was typical of the smaller lumber schooners and when new must have been as beautiful in her own way as the lovely French empress who made the name popular in the seventies and eighties. A graceful elliptical stern and long cutwater decorated with carved billet head and trailboards distinguished her, and right up to the end, she looked like a little clipper with two topmasts aloft and a long flying jibboom thrusting out eagerly ahead of her. When I first knew her, the master was Captain Ed Davis of Machias, a kindly old man who had been on the coast for a lifetime. One trip, off Thacher's Island with several vessels in company bound to Lynn, we saw the *Eugenie* suddenly bear off and go into Gloucester. A few days later, Johnny Forhan, the mate, brought her into Lynn and told us that old Cap'n Davis had dropped dead that day, collapsing on deck without a word.

Later on, Sant Lloyd, who had been in the *Alice S. Wentworth* and later the *Frank Brainerd* with Captain Stevens, took over the *Eugenie* with Bert Deshon of Portland, who was a comparative newcomer to the coasting fleet, having spent much of his time in fishermen. I joined her later and the reunion with Sant was a pleasant one.

The *Eugenie* was one of those schooners that originally carried several hands in a forecastle in the forward house, long since

45. Galley of the schooner *Eugenie.* Located in the port forward corner of the after deckhouse, it was the source of much good but inexpensive food. There is a slack salted pollock hanging from a nail behind the stove. The author's berth is at the left.

become the home of the donkey engine and pumps. The engine was hooked up to the windlass by a heavy sprocket chain that passed through a slot in the forward bulkhead of the deckhouse, and the winchheads projected from each side. She handled well, steered easily, and was a pleasure to sail.

All three of us slept aft, Sant and Bert having two small staterooms, a third room having been eliminated when some of the partitions were torn out to make the cabin more light and roomy. One berth had been left as a sort of sofa and this was mine. A galley was arranged in the port forward corner of the deckhouse, and a large kitchen table was fastened to the bulkhead to starboard. A couple of comfortable chairs, plenty of gimballed lamps, and a Boston terrier pup created a comfortable and home-like atmosphere.

On the last trip I made with them, we were chartered to load boxboards at Back River off the Sheepscot where a portable sawmill had been set up. Coming in from outside, the wind died out when we were off Seguin, so we put the yawl-boat over and finished the passage with the old Knox one-lunger banging away under the stern. Up the river and around the end of Barter's Island we went then down the Back River to a crude temporary wharf of poles projected into the stream.

Obviously we would be grounding out at low tide, but the lumber shipper assured us it was a soft mud bottom so we hauled in, ran our lines ashore, and left a kedge anchor off in the stream on a long line. It was too late in the day to begin loading so we went below for supper. The tide was ebbing and suddenly we began to hear strange noises — creaking and cracking and before we realized what it meant, the whole wheelbox lifted off the deck, pushed up by the rudder head. Rushing on deck we found that as the *Eugenie* fetched up on the bottom, instead of soft mud there was ledge and rock just below the surface and she was hung up hard and fast at either end. A boulder right under the heel of the rudder forced it upward, unshipping it and tearing the wheelbox adrift. Worse yet, the mastheads began to lean toward each other and the spring stay drooped between them. This indicated that what soft mud there was lay right amidships, leaving the hull unsupported there. Looking over the side we found the oakum hanging festooned from the seams, squeezed out by the pressure. Although the *Eugenie* was not as badly hogged as some of the other schooners, she had straightened out a lot in her forty-odd years and now, for a time, it looked as though she was about to regain her original sheer. At last the tide came in sufficiently to float her again but it was touch and go whether we could keep her afloat or not. We had in the meantime been doing some probing in the mud and shifted her to a new berth where she laid easily. On the next low tide, we got over the side and hawsed the caulking back into the seams and did what we could to tighten her up. The worst of the leaking was over but she was never as tight again as she had been before the accident.

That fall after I had left to spend some time ashore in an attempt to renew a school career, the *Eugenie* piled ashore near Small Point during a heavy gale. Sant, Bert, and the dog got safely ashore, although they almost froze to death before finding shelter. The schooner was a total loss, for in a few hours she had completely disintegrated.

46. The rocky Maine coast is a poor place for a vessel to be ashore. When the *Eugenie* stranded near Small Point, it was on a black night and during a northeast gale. With the vessel breaking up under their feet, Sant Lloyd, Bert Deshon, and the small Boston terrier mascot could only crawl out to the end of the flying jibboom and drop, hoping to land on terra firma. They did — in water up to their waists — and nearly froze before they found shelter.

10 | THE ALICE S. WENTWORTH

I suppose every man (or boy) who ever went to sea had a favorite vessel. Mine was the then handsome *Alice S. Wentworth*. She is still afloat as a tourist attraction beside a Boston waterfront restaurant, but she now bears little resemblance to the beautifully sheered and smart little coaster she was in 1920.

Originally the *Lizzie A. Tolles,* built at South Norwalk, Connecticut, in 1863, she was bought by the Stevens family in the early nineties. Her new home port was Wells, although she hailed from Kennebunk and later, Portland. After the turn of the century, she was owned wholly by Captain Arthur A. Stevens. In 1904, he hauled her up on the bank at Wells and completely rebuilt her. Owning a sawmill engaged in sawing ship timber, he didn't skimp on material and renewed everything that showed signs of being in poor condition.

The centerboard and case were replaced, new keelsons added, deck and deck frames renewed, stem and stern rebuilt, and many new planks and frames added. When finished she was the practical equivalent of a new vessel and under the law was entitled to a complete new documentation. This was issued in 1905 and she became the *Alice S. Wentworth,* named for Captain Stevens' favorite niece, since he had no children of his own.

A deep sheer was the vessel's outstanding characteristic and it was accentuated by the two yellow stripes around the hull, one along a bead moulding about 2 inches below the main rail and the other at the planksheer, just below the level of the main deck. Her wide, deeply raked transom was ornamented by a carved eagle, and her cutwater swept gracefully forward terminating in a carved billet head supported by headrails and carved trailboards. She was painted a dark moss green from waterline to planksheer and had a black bulwark above it. She was launched with only a main topmast aloft but a foretopmast was soon added. With a main boom of about 60 feet in length and a gaff in proportion, she set a big mainsail and with both topsails, a fisherman staysail, and a jib topsail set, she could spread enough canvas to catch any vagrant breeze that rippled the water. For a coaster, she was fast, and it is safe to say that in her prime she was one of the smartest vessels of her size along the coast. Certainly nothing in her class ever passed her while I knew her.

47. The *Alice S. Wentworth* in the Webhannet River at Wells, Maine. Author's collection.

48. The *Alice S. Wentworth* deep-loaded with coal, running into the Webhannet River in a dirty southeaster. Author's collection.

Captain Stevens was a man of many affairs and frequently went home, leaving the *Alice* in the capable hands of his mate, Sant Lloyd. Sant and I made several trips two-handed, for with a good hoisting engine forward and power in the yawl-boat, she was easily handled as such vessels go.

As in most small coasters, all hands slept in the after house which contained four berths, a stove and counters, and dish lockers against the forward bulkhead. Seat lockers extended in front of the two berths on each side and partly across the after bulkhead to provide a landing place for the companionway ladder. A kitchen table covered with red tablecloth was fixed against the after bulkhead, and a couple of ordinary kitchen chairs completed the furnishings except for the gimballed lamps on the forward and after bulkheads. The cabin floor was maple to match the paneling above the bunks, and it was kept as clean as regular scrubbing with water and sand could make it. Unlike most down-east vessels, there were ports in the sides of the cabin rather than square windows, but there was a large skylight overhead and in all but the most bitterly cold or rainy weather, the companionway was left open. With a good wood fire in the stove, the cabin was almost too warm, even on cold days.

When Captain Stevens was aboard, he had the starboard forward bunk, apparently preferring it to the after one which was his by tradition. He was a quiet, somewhat moody man, given to long silences broken occasionally by unpredictable fits of verbosity. He was never "onery," however, and much of the time he was aboard, acted almost more like a guest than the master. He would sit on the wheelbox sometimes for hours, saying hardly a word

49. My berth in the *Alice S. Wentworth's* after house. A snug place
to be on a cold winter night.

50. Left to right: the author, aged fifteen; his seven-year-old sister, Syrena, visiting aboard at Lynn; and Sant Lloyd, mate. Author's collection.

until suddenly he would break into speech or sing a meaningless little ditty in a voice like the squeak of a rusty hinge. One of his favorites was something about "Johnny Morgan played the organ, Sister played the drum . . . " He never finished it so I never learned any more about the musical accomplishments of Johnny and his sister. After such an outburst the old man would grin rather sheepishly and retire into silence for a protracted period.

Sant (his name was Santford) was much more companionable, although he was never what might be termed loquacious. A former deepwater sailor, he was neat as an old-maid housekeeper and could make a stab at cooking like one also. He had a hand like a smoked ham and fingers as big as the butt end of a marlin spike but what he could do with them was amazing. He had a passion for fixing clocks and since we happened to have two aboard, he was always taking one or the other apart. He was an expert at marlin spike seamanship and an effective teacher of fancy rope work and knot tying, as I once found out — the hard way.

He had undertaken the task of teaching me to make fourteen-strand flat sinnet, but I couldn't seem to get the hang of it and finally flung it down impatiently. We were sitting on the heel of the bowsprit at the time and Sant quietly told me to pick it up and finish it. I demurred and said it wasn't worth the trouble. Again, he insisted that I pick it up and get on with it. I said, "Oh to hell with it," and stood up to go aft. As I did so, he came to his feet and his fist connected with my jaw. When I came to I was stretched out on deck aft of the windlass, getting a bucket of seawater in the face and a prod in the ribs from Sant's number ten boot. "Now," he drawled, "get back and finish that sinnet!" Needless to say, I put up no further argument and from that day to this, I have never quite forgotten how to make fourteen-strand sinnet.

Easygoing in disposition, he was strong as a bull and woe to anyone who forced trouble on him. A drunken longshoreman tried to force a fight on him one night in a little waterfront restaurant. Sant ignored him at first but when the fellow took a swing at him, Sant ducked and slapped him open-handed, opening his cheek almost to the bone. The would-be battler ran suddenly out of steam.

Once, when I was furling the flying jib, the footrope I was standing on broke and I dropped into the water under the bow. It was winter and I was dressed in heavy clothes under well-lashed oilskins. Fortunately the vessel was making just enough headway so I managed to get my arms around the bobchains as I fought my way to the surface. I was, by then, so waterlogged I could only hang on. Sant had seen me fall and came running forward. Climbing down on the bobchains, and holding on with one hand, he got his fingers in the collars of my oilskin jacket and clothing and giving one tremendous yank, lifted me up beside him. I weighed close to 180 pounds at the time and, with my wet clothes, must have totaled another 15 pounds or more above that.

It was a happy life in the *Wentworth*. We seemed to have no difficulties in getting good cargoes both ways. Many old coasters in later years were forced to go back east light, but seldom did the *Alice* sail without an eastbound cargo of salt, coal, or coke for some eastern port.

Salt was the favorite, of course, for it was clean and easily loaded — when there were at least two of us aboard. Once it happened otherwise. We had been chartered to load salt out of a Dutch steamer at Gloucester, just in from Turk's Island. The cargo was destined for a fish packing plant at Boothbay. We had discharged a load of boxboards at Lynn, and the old man had gone home to Wells, leaving us two-handed to take the vessel east. Arriving at Gloucester, we hauled alongside the steamer, already discharging part of her cargo at one of the wharves and were told it would be next day before they were ready to load us. Thereupon, Sant went uptown to do some shopping leaving me alone as shipkeeper.

A short time after he had gone, the mate of the steamer yelled over the side that operations had been suspended ashore and they might as well load us. The fact that I was all alone was disregarded. Chutes were slung into each of our two hatches and the winches began to clatter as bucket after bucket of salt was emptied into the hold. Grabbing a shovel, I jumped below and went desperately to work in an attempt to trim out the cargo fore and aft, but despite my best efforts, I couldn't keep pace with the double stream of salt that came hurtling down. It wasn't long before the stuff was choking the hatches and piling up on deck. When Sant arrived back aboard, we had several hours of backbreaking work to shovel the surplus below.

It was that trip when we had the pleasure of beating a big schooner yacht on the run down east. With a light load of salt under hatches, the *Wentworth* was in good sailing trim. Getting under way from the inner harbor, we cleared Eastern Point and headed for the Londoner Buoy off Thacher's Island. As we came up to it, the yacht, also bound east, passed us swiftly in the light air then prevailing. On the after deck a group of guests who had obviously been enjoying liquid refreshment waved and yelled a few dubious pleasantries. We were helpless and had to watch them increase the lead over us until they were a couple of miles or so ahead.

Before long, however, the wind — which had been light sou'westerly — began to cant more to the south and east and breeze on in ever increasing gusts. We had the topsails set and decided to let them stand, although they should have really come in with only the two of us aboard. The topmasts were soon bending like coachwhips and with the lee scuppers buried deep in foam, we drove hard to the eastward, the bluff bow shouldering the darkening sea into a smother of white water. With the wind aft of the beam, it was a constant fight against the kicking wheel, but Sant held her steady as we began to overhaul the yacht ahead of us. Before dark we passed her floundering under a foresail and fore staysail, while we roared by to windward with both topsails still standing — although for how long, we didn't know. It was going to be touch and go whether we could get them in before they blew out or the topmasts went, but with the aid of the power winch I managed to get both sails clewed up in the gear and climbed aloft to pass the gaskets. It took about an hour but at last I had them frapped into the mastheads and came down to give Sant some respite from the wheel while he made some sandwiches for supper. By this time the wind had steadied and all night it kept our lee scuppers under and the hawsepipes spouting as the schooner ran off to the no'theast. Next day we were in Boothbay with our cargo partly discharged when the yacht came drooping in, still under short canvas with only one or two of her people sitting dispiritedly on deck as she made the anchorage.

In those days yachtsmen, even those who sailed, were regarded with some condescension for they were still a race apart. Conrad, in writing of the meeting of a group of men who began life in the merchant service, alluded to "the fellowship of the craft which no amount of enthusiasm for yachting, cruising and so on can give, since one is only the amusement of life and the other is life itself." Perhaps it was something of this idea which inspired the impoverished skipper of a broken-down coaster to sneer at the uniformed and brass-bound Deer Isle master of a big yacht, "Damn fool — that's all he's good fur — to go yachtin'!" (Although I am sure he had never read Conrad). This, despite the fact that the yacht skipper was no less a good seaman and probably made twice as much money and had a dozen well-trained men in his crew to relieve him of the arduous work.

The *Wentworth* never lacked for cargoes and there was hardly a loading port she didn't visit. Up the Sheepscot river to Wiscasset she went to load at the wharf where now lie the wrecks of the *Luther Little* and the *Hesper*. Further east, her bow breasted the gently flowing waters of the Georges River above the bridge at Thomaston between the dark trees of the upper stream until she lay alongside the old road bridge at South Warren. Here the lumber was loaded from teams which paused briefly on the bridge and then turned back up country for more. At Lincolnville Beach she chafed her sides impatiently against the piling of the almost unprotected wharf, and at Sargentville she lay placidly at the old steamboat wharf waiting for the teamloads of boxboards which made up the cargo. Further east, she sailed up Dyer's Bay inside Petit Manan to load far up from open water, her lines made fast to the trees on the creek bank. Here she was almost tide-nipped, and just managed to scrape through the mud on the last of a high run of tides to get clear again.

That was a long hard trip, and it was well into February before we headed up Lynn Harbor channel in Massachusetts on the last leg of the passage. Bitterly cold weather, gales, and a series of mishaps slowed her down and days were spent at anchor first in one harbor, then another, waiting for the weather to improve. By Christmas she had only reached Port Clyde and when it finally did look like clearing weather with a good chance along, the old man shaped a course outside, determined to try for Cape Ann in one big jump. Back went the wind into the northeast, however, and we made Portland Lightship just before the thickening snow cut off all visibility.

It was useless to keep going under such conditions and Captain Stevens swung her off for Portland, still hanging on to all plain sail. There was a saying along the coast that refuge in Portland meant ten days at anchor and many coasting skippers hated to go in for that reason, but in this case there was no choice. We took our departure from the lightship and prayed the compass was not too far out. Wind-driven snow shut out the rest of the world and there was no means of checking the course. Too far to the westward and we might fetch up on Trundy's Reef. Too far to the eastward and Ram Island ledges might tear her bottom out.

On we ran, wondering if the sails and gear would hold. Not a glimmer showed anywhere as we drove blindly through a mael-strom of sleet, wind, and icy spray, freezing almost instantane-oulsy as it hit. Suddenly, after what seemed like an eternity, a light flashed dimly through the snow high up on our port hand. It had to be Portland Head, for if it had been anything else we would have already been pounding our bottom out on the ledges. The old man checked the course and before long we made Spring Point light and then the breakwater. Gybing over, we hauled up and ran under the sterns of several other schooners already lying safely with anchors down and riding lights gleaming faintly through the snow. We cleared them all and rounded up, letting go both anchors as we sagged to leeward away from the gale that was now howling at top strength. Forty-five fathoms of chain went over the windlass before she rode easily under the lee of the South Portland shore. Then came the fight to get the ice-coated sails down and stowed, well gasketted against the wind that plucked hungrily at any loose gear.

It was three days before we could get ashore with the assistance of a towboat skipper, an excoasterman who made the rounds of the fleet to give a lift to those who wanted to stretch their legs on terra firma and do some shopping to replenish diminished larders.

A frostbitten face served to remind me of that night for many years afterward, for always thereafter, a cold wind roused pain in my cheeks that was like a toothache.

For weeks we lay straining at our anchor chains and nothing moved on the coast except a few big steamers that came and went, their whistles hooting and bellowing as they groped their way in and out of the long channel. The old man went home to Wells,

51. The *Alice S. Wentworth* at Hoague, Sprague's wharf at Lynn.
Author's collection.

and Sant and I settled down to cribbage and other time-killing pursuits while the days and nights blended one into the other until all sense of time was lost. Every morning Sant would get out of his bunk at daylight, stick his head up through the companionway — and crawl back into his blankets, cursing the weather.

Once in a while we would try to break away some of the ice that had accumulated on the bobchains and coated the whole fore part of the schooner in a frosting inches thick. Other than that, there was nothing to do except wait. We almost wished she would start leaking so we could pump, but hardly a drop of water did she make and a few strokes now and then sufficed to keep her free.

At last the break came and a large fleet streamed out by the cape in the wintry sunshine. Some stood boldly across for the tip of Cape Cod while others, bound to Boston only, hugged the shore ready to dodge in at the first sign of bad weather.

This time we managed to make Kittery, and next morning when the wind still hung in the nor'westerly quadrant we got under way and headed across for Thacher's Island to "turn the corner" of Cape Ann. It was a fair wind right aft, but because of the long spell of easterlies before the clearing shift, a big ground swell set into Ipswich Bay from abeam as the fleet went rolling down across, dipping their deckloads with spars swaying wildly across the cold blue sky.

"Wung out" with the foresail on one side and the mainsail on the other, we ran off before the fresh nor'wester with boom tackles taut and the helmsman sweating blood at the wheel trying to keep her on course. I was steering when I sensed, rather than heard, the crack of something parting and as she rolled back over

52. "Wung out" with a boom tackle rigged on the main to prevent gybing. The tackle was carried slung between beckets under the main boom, and when in use, was hooked into the long pennant (usually wire) which led aft from an eye bolt in the rail just aft of the fore rigging. The pennant was tethered to the main rigging near its end by a short stopper or tricing line. The hauling part of the tackle was made fast on a pin in the jaws of the main boom, usually the one on which the topsail tack or sheet might be made fast also.

THE ALICE S. WENTWORTH | 99

the swell, the big main boom lifted and swooped across in a standing gybe. The wire boom tackle pennant from the fore rigging had parted and the tackle itself caught in the after corner of the deckload, ripping it loose and causing several hundred feet of lumber to go overboard. I dropped to the deck as the main sheet and boom tackle snaked over my head and the boom fetched up with a tremendous crash at the end of the roll. I expected to see the main boom in pieces or the sail in ribbons, but somehow everything held. Hauling her up a little more on the wind to prevent another gybe, we made a temporary boom tackle pennant with a double part of towing hawser and finished the passage across the bay.

Captain Stevens sold the *Alice S. Wentworth* to Captain Zeb Tilton and others of Vineyard Haven, Massachusetts, in 1921, buying the handsome three-master *Frank Brainerd* to replace her. It seemed a good move at first, but after a while troubles began to accumulate. There were rumors of financial difficulties at home and later, when the *Brainerd* grounded in Frenchman's Bay after loading for New York, he was unable to meet the salvage bills without borrowing heavily on the schooner. None of the coasters in those last years carried hull insurance, for the cost would have been prohibitive even if they had been able to find someone to write it. Ownership of the *Brainerd* eventually passed to Merritt Ober of Rockland, and Captain Stevens took over the Providence-owned *Altana M. Jagger,* sailing on shares around Long Island Sound and Narragansett Bay.

He apparently made a living in her although hardly more than that. I have a memorandum of the *Jagger's* accounts for the year 1928 received from Captain Fred C. Smith, a former master who kept a share in the schooner after leaving her. It was submitted by Allen Gurney, the Providence ship broker and agent who was the managing owner at the time. On his letterhead, it is made out as follows:

January 9, 1929

Memorandum accounts, schooner *Altana M. Jagger* for 1928.

Balance from 1927 account		$ 307.68
Gross stock	$5,830.56	
Port charges	$1,192.53	
Net stock	$4,638.03	
Capt.'s share [Stevens]	$2,553.94	
Vessel's share	$2,084.09	
Bank interest	$ 0.76	$2,084.85
		$2,392.53
Less vessel's bills	$1,364.17	
Man'g. owner fee	$ 75.00	
Dividend No. 51	$ 640.00	$2,079.17
		$ 313.36

From this it would appear the *Jagger* was paying her way, but it is equally obvious she paid small dividends to her owners. Captain Stevens was apparently unable to save much from his earnings, for I later heard that he died in poor circumstances.

11 | VETERANS OF THE COAST

In a mechanized age of steel and machines, of new materials and methods, it is amazing to recall what men once did with wood and iron, working only with their hands and a few simple tools. Some of the vessels they built lasted for incredible lengths of time and, in the end, disintegrated from neglect rather than from sheer old age.

Back in 1833 a little 82-ton two-masted coaster was launched at Belfast under the name of *Catherine*. Ninety years later she was still struggling back and forth in Penobscot Bay carrying box-boards from Somesville to Rockland. Her sagging hull and blackened spars made her a pitiful looking object, and she looked every year of her age. Even so, she had retained her shape better than many, and had a little more been spent on her from time to time during the late years, there is small doubt she would have passed the century mark. However, she finally gave out while waiting to load at Somesville and her timbers are in the mud there still.

The *Lulu W. Eppes,* which I joined after leaving the *George W. Collins,* had originally been built as the schooner *Red Rover*

at Kingston, Massachusetts, in 1837. There were stories along the coast that in her early years she had operated almost entirely in the Gulf Coast area and had been engaged in slave-running from the Cuban barracoons to American gulf ports. She was then owned by a Massachusetts South Shore family who were said to have become ardent abolitionists during the Civil War. If she ever had been a slaver, she must have delivered her cargoes by stealth rather than speed, for when I was in her she was the dullest sailer in the bay and an awkward tub to handle under any conditions. She had come down east in the eighties, and in 1898 was rebuilt by Dan Eppes at Ellsworth, receiving new documentation and being renamed for his wife. For many years she was operated by Whitcomb, Haynes & Whitney before she was laid up in Contention Cove at Surry for lack of business. Following World War I the demand for vessels to carry boxboards inspired Captain Freeman Closson to refit her as best he could and put her back to work once more after making a deal with the owners to sail her on shares. He had previously been master of the *Ann C. Stuart,* after having had the *Lois M. Candage* for about fifteen years.

53. The old *Catherine,* ninety-year-old veteran of the coast, on one of her last trips. Courtesy John Quincy Adams.

The owners were not optimistic and apparently didn't care to make any major expenditures for refitting, but by dint of a lot of hard work and the use of secondhand gear salvaged from other old vessels, Freeman got her going again and took her up to Somesville to load boxboards for Rockland.

There was no hoisting engine with which to handle sails and anchors and, instead of a yawl-boat, a dory hung on the stern davits. Like any old schooner whose seams had become hollowed from constant caulking to the point where they could no longer retain the oakum, the *Eppes* was made tight by the liberal use of "gump wedges." These were wooden strips (sometimes laths) planed narrower on one edge and driven into gaping seams like a spline and sometimes secured with shingle nails. Coal tar and canvas patches were plastered over rotten butts and hood ends of planking to keep the water from running in faster than it could be pumped out. The job on the *Eppes* was a pretty effective one and she needed comparatively little pumping while I was in her. She was not sailed hard and merely drifted from harbor to harbor, so in the comparatively short period of her resurrection she didn't have the chance to work loose again. Her appearance, however, was almost as bad as that of the old *Catherine*. No money had been spent for paint except a little inside white for the cabin, and her hull was mottled and weatherbeaten. With canvas patches and blobs of coal tar spotted over her sides, she resembled a seagoing hobo.

Her after house, nevertheless, was as tidy and homelike as a good housekeeper like Bertha Closson could make it. She always accompanied her husband in the vessels he had and in the *Eppes*,

54. The *Lulu W. Eppes,* old and tired but a happy home afloat with Captain Freeman Closson and his Nantucket wife Bertha. Author's collection.

the quarters were as snug as their farm kitchen at Bayside. There were crisp little curtains at the windows and even a cheerful geranium to lend a dash of color to the stark whiteness of the fresh paint.

Bertha was a Nantucket girl where good cooks are the rule rather than the exception, and had there been a Duncan Hines of the coast, I am sure he would have nominated her as "woman of the year" in the field of culinary achievement. Although diminutive in size, she could hold turn on a halyard as well as anyone and take a trick at the wheel if necessary, but it was at the cookstove that her finest talents became manifest. What she could do with cheap cuts of meat, fish and a few vegetables would have made a gourmet's mouth water. The memory of her fried bread, "riz" biscuits, and flavorful stews, chowders and meat pies haunts me to this day.

Getting the *Eppes* under way with no h'ister was a long, slow, and backbreaking process. On our last passage in her, we had come across the Bay from Rockland, bound for Somesville again, but had anchored in Fox Island Thoroughfare over night. Next morning we finally managed to get the four lowers on her and started along the waterway toward Iron Point. Just before fetching the spindle, one of the old main sheet blocks partially gave way and the sheet jammed between the sheave and the shell. The wind was drawing off the Vinalhaven shore and with the mainsheet well in and jammed, she began to luff as we struggled frantically to clear it so we could get her to keep off. In the middle of this, the skipper, who had been ruptured for years, gave a cry of pain and dropped to the deck. By the time Bertha and I pulled

him out of the way, the vessel had shot up into the wind and before we could do anything about it, was entangled with a large float in front of a summer cottage on the Vinalhaven side of the Thoroughfare. There was nothing to do but let the sails come down on the run and hail a passing fisherman for assistance. He towed us out into Kent's Cove where we anchored and then got the skipper below and into a bunk. There he declared that he'd be all right in a day or two but he sent me ashore to send a telegram to his younger brother, Irving, at Ellsworth.

Since we had no power yawl-boat, I landed on the beach that rimmed the cove and started across the field to reach the road. I soon realized the field was a grazing ground for a large herd of sheep and suddenly became aware of a large ram who was obviously preparing to drive out intruders. I gauged the distance to the nearest section of fence and started toward it, keeping a wary eye on the ram. Suddenly he started for me and we made a race of it to the fence. I won and scrambled ingloriously over it at the cost of a pair of torn dungarees and severe injury to my dignity. He glared balefully at me from behind the bars and I made up my mind that if he was in the same place when I got back, my approach to the beach would have to be circuitous. So it proved to be when I got back from town a couple of hours later. There he was in almost the same place, waiting grimly. I backed away and made a wide circle to the point where the fence ran down to the beach. I climbed over it there and headed up the beach to the boat. I was about half way there when he apparently spotted me or wandered into range by chance. Once more he sounded his "tally ho" and came after me with hooves pounding and horns lowered. I made a wild dash for the boat and casting the painter adrift, pushed off the beach into icy water up to my waist. He did not follow me in but it was easy to see that a new landing spot would have to be chosen for any subsequent trips ashore.

Irving showed up in a couple of days, but by that time, a spell of easterly weather had set in and it was days before we were able to get out of the cove. We spent the time checking and repairing the rest of the blocks and various odd jobs. One day after starting aloft to check the blocks at the masthead, two ratlines broke under me in succession and I fell back down against the rigging and shot off into the water. I hit the cold water with a mighty splash, a little stunned, but somehow managed to swim to the bow where Irving helped me aboard via the bob chains. Fortunately, I was not really injured but I had landed spread-eagled on my back with sufficient force to drive the blood out through the skin. My back was red as a boiled lobster and I was lame and sore for days afterward. Freeman, by now, was able to get out on deck and by the time the sou'westers returned, was able to take the wheel while Irving and I, with Bertha's assistance, got the sails set and the vessel under way for Union River Bay. Once home, Freeman had the family doctor come in but operations were not as common then as they are now and he was forced to rest up for quite a spell. Meanwhile arrangements had been made to sell the vessel and we were stranded ashore, willy-nilly. Some time later, I heard the *M. M. Hamilton* was loading at Somesville, so off I went, headed toward home — I hoped.

The new owner of the *Eppes* took her to Rockland, had her hauled on Snow's railway, and gave orders to have her put in good condition. Gump wedges were pulled out, gaping seams reefed out and recaulked and structural repairs made where necessary. Several weeks and a couple of thousand dollars later she was launched again, resplendent in new paint, sails, and gear. However, it wasn't long before she showed signs of "spitting her caulking" once more and she was sold to go south, to the West Indies, it was reported. Bad luck dogged her, however, and she got ashore in Narragansett Bay. For a time it looked as though she had reached the end of her career. She was salvaged, however, but she never reached the Caribbean. Instead, she wound up in Chesapeake Bay in the Virginia-Baltimore lumber trade. There she continued to operate for several more years before she was abandoned.

The champion of all coasters in the matter of age was the 48-ton *Polly*, built at Amesbury in 1805. For years a legend persisted that she had been a privateer in the War of 1812. In fact, a female patriotic organization known as the Daughters of the War of 1812 had a bronze plaque made and mounted on the vessel's cabin attesting to what they insisted was a fact. The plaque may now be seen at the Penobscot Marine Museum in Searsport, Maine.

In April, 1944, this myth was exploded by John R. Herbert of the *Quincy Patriot-Ledger,* who did a complete piece of research on the history of the ancient vessel. His findings were published in the *American Neptune,* a quarterly journal of maritime history published at the Peabody Museum in Salem, Massachusetts. Although she was not a privateer, the *Polly's* active career did cover a period of 113 years. So far as is known, this is second in longevity to the record of the little ship *True Love* of 296 tons, built in Phil-

adelphia in 1764 and still working in Hull, England, in 1888, a span of 124 years.

The *Polly's* first document indicated she was built as a sloop at Amesbury, Massachusetts, in 1805 and that she continued with that rig until about 1861 when she was rebuilt by Jonathan Tinker at Bluehill, Maine. A document issued April 20, 1865, shows her home port to be Southwest Harbor and her rig that of a schooner. She was later owned by Lewis Arey of South Thomaston for many years before being sold to Portland. Thereafter, she changed owners several times and hailed from Rockland, Belfast, Deer Isle, and at last from Fall River, Massachusetts, although continuing to operate in the Maine lumber trade. At one time she also carried lime and, occasionally, stone. On her last trip the *Polly* brought a load of lumber to Quincy, but she was in such poor condition by then that she was laid up in the Town River to await repairs. They were never made, however, and after further deterioration, she was broken up.

Not many years before the First World War there were still other very old vessels washing about the coast, although none quite so ancient as the *Polly*. Her immediate runners-up were the *Good Intent* built at Braintree, Massachusetts, in 1813 and the *Hiram*, launched at Biddeford, Maine, in 1819.

The *Good Intent* seldom left Penobscot Bay in her later years, being operated principally as a "kiln-wooder." She was a little thing of only 24 tons, owned in Bucksport.

The *Hiram* was a better-known vessel in the general coasting trade, having been engaged in carrying lumber and hay from the Bangor River to Boston and lumber and stone from Calais, Vinal-haven, and St. George. During the course of her active career she was rebuilt extensively but she, too, seemed to change but little in appearance. She was bluff-bowed and square-sterned with wooden boat davits and a high box rail around her poop. Although she registered only 67 tons, she had originally carried several hands and retained her forecastle house until her last days. Like many of the older schooners, she had very little sheer but what she did have she seemed to keep comparatively well.

After changing owners and hailing ports many times, the *Hiram* came into possession of Captain Jimmy Orne, a widely known character along the coast. He always took his wife Georgie with him and it was asserted by many, including her, that she was the real master of the vessel. When they purchased the vessel in 1912, stories got into the newspapers that the old vessel was to be fitted out for a voyage around Cape Horn to be present at the San Francisco Exposition in 1915. Further publicity followed when the *Hiram* arrived at Boston, and pictures of the whole family appeared in the Boston dailies including numerous yarns about the projected Cape Horn trip. The reporters had a field day for a while, for "Captain Georgie" proclaimed her authority in the many interviews and poor old Jimmy was relegated to the status of deckhand. Their daughter Lillian was cook, and when questioned about her lack of opportunity for schooling, the parents declared that she got sick every time she went ashore so it was necessary for them to keep her with them aboard the schooner at all times. Needless to say, the Cape Horn trip never came off, and the *Hiram* eventually ended her days in one of the backwaters of Boston Harbor.

55. The ancient *Polly,* built in 1805 and still sailing 113 years later. From a Stebbins negative in the Peabody Museum, Salem, Massachusetts.

56. The schooner *Robert W.* on I. L. Snow's railway at Rockland,
Maine, beside a Finnish bark. Courtesy Peabody Museum, Salem,
Massachusetts.

Another old-timer, the two-masted *Robert W.,* laid her bones on York Beach in 1923. Built at Piermont, New York, in 1847, she passed through several changes of name and a long coasting career. She was launched under the name of *Entire,* and after changing owners some time later, was renamed *Robert A. Kinnier.* She came down east about the turn of the century and hailed from Bangor under the last of the three names she bore. She was later owned in Winterport but in 1920 was sold to the Red Beach Plaster Co. for about $3,500. About a year later, however, she was sold at auction by a U.S. marshal and was bid in by I. L. Snow & Co. of Rockland for only $870. January, 1923, found her loading boxboards at Thomaston for Lynn.

Manned by Captain B. F. Mitchell and his son Stanley, she sailed for Boston, a hard chance for a short-handed 91-ton schooner. On the morning of January 12 a northeast gale with heavy snow enveloped the New England coast, but during a momentary lift of the snow curtain in the evening, watchers at York Beach were startled to see a two-masted schooner lying well over on her beam ends in the breaking seas several hundred yards offshore. The news soon spread around town, and a crowd quickly gathered and a huge bonfire was built. Nothing could be done at the time although two men could plainly be seen, lashed in the rigging and coated with snow and frozen spray. Later on, the gale having abated and the tide receded on the ebb, rescuers reached the doomed vessel and brought the frost-bitten and helpless men ashore. The schooner proved to be the *Robert W.,* which had been running for the shelter of Portsmouth Harbor when the breakers were discovered almost under her bow. With no room to maneuver she struck directly and was driven hard onto the sand.

So they disappeared, one by one, victims of time, weather, and neglect. They were like the veterans of a war, lasting about so long and then coming to their ends in a short span of years.

57. Captain Parker J. Hall taking the *Alice S. Wentworth* out of Nantucket after purchasing her about July 1943. He was then about eighty-two years old. Courtesy Charles F. Sayle.

58. Captain Parker J. Hall about 1910, at the wheel of the little schooner *Mizpah,* which he owned briefly. He was already becoming a legendary character along the coast. Courtesy of Charles Sayle.

12 | SOME SKIPPERS

"SHIPS are all right," said a character of Joseph Conrad's, "it's the men in 'em," and so it is: good men, bad men, indifferent and sometimes incompetent — although seldom the latter for long.

There were all kinds of men in the coasters, the large majority being competent but undistinguished. Some, however, for one reason or another were known all along the coast. Many I remember. Others had departed long before I ever came to the coasters although now and then one or another was remembered and his exploits recalled by some of his brother captains.

Certainly in the time I remember, the outstanding character of them all was Captain Parker J. Hall of Sandy Point. He was not a down easter by birth for he was born on the south shore of Massachusetts Bay and did not come to Maine to make his home until he was well into middle age, although most of his coasting career was carried on in the waters between Cape Cod and the Maine ports of call.

No one seemed to know exactly how old he was, for with regard to some things he could be very mysterious. I suppose there is a record somewhere, but to my knowledge no one ever got a true idea of his age from Parker. According to the best calcula-tions, he was born sometime prior to the Civil War, for he had been coasting in the heyday of the trade and was a gold mine of information about the skippers, crews, and vessels of other years. Legends were built around him during his lifetime, and he did nothing to discourage them. His stuttering was like machine-gun fire and there were even stories about that. He was reported to have met other men similarly afflicted on several occasions, and since Parker was notoriously short-tempered, the incidents were not devoid of excitement.

His chief claim to fame, however, was his single-handed sailing. He might take passengers, but never in the years down east did he carry a paid hand. Some of the vessels he owned and sailed were big schooners as such craft go and it was a source of much wonder how he managed it. He was, of course, tremendously strong and extraordinarily capable as a seaman, but even other coastermen who were used to going short-handed were amazed at times to see what Parker could do all by himself.

His refusal to carry a crew stemmed from an incident in the *Robert P. King,* a 119-ton two-master of which he was master in the early 1900s. His crew of three men attacked him with the object of robbing him of his newly collected freight money. He killed one of them and put the other two to rout, being wounded himself in the process. He was cleared of any blame in the affair but thereafter he always went single handed. He continued in the *King,* despite the fact that she was a "hand-puller" with no power for handling the anchors or sails nor any power in the yawl-boat. In later years when he had the old *Angler* out of Duxbury, he had his wife with him for a time but later still, he bought the *George R. Smith,* which was even larger than the *King* had been, and went back to his solitary voyaging. The *Smith* had been built at Orrington, Maine, as the *Nellie Doe* in 1867 and registered about 130 tons. She was rebuilt and renamed some time in the nineties and was finally lost by fire at Duxbury, Massachusetts, about 1922. For a time Parker had the *Carrie,* a little bay coaster which was distinctive for her plumb stem. He lost her in peculiar fashion at Mackerel Cove when he anchored there for the night and at low tide the vessel settled down on some abandoned weir stakes which punctured her bottom. Parker awoke in time to get away from her before she filled and sank, but she never came off bottom. Another little schooner, the *Howard Russell,* which he operated in the bay coasting business, capsized at Swan's Island.

He next bought the *George Gress,* a former Hudson River "bricker" of 64 tons, built at Athens, New York, in 1885 as the *Peter Merhoff,* bringing her down east from the Connecticut River where she had been working. She must have been a handsome little schooner originally for she was beautifully decorated around the bow and stern, although in her later years she was badly hogged. He continued in her for some years with only a cat as

crew, and then sold her to a couple of young fellows who were new at the business. They entered the pulpwood trade with her just before the outbreak of the last war but she got ashore and became a total loss.

Parker bought the old *William C. Pendleton* where she lay on the mud at Pulpit Harbor, and with the aid of plenty of oakum, gump wedges, and coal tar, made her tight enough to float once more. She resumed her old trade as a bay coaster although Parker only kept her for a short time.

His last vessel was the *Alice S. Wentworth,* which he bought from Zeb Tilton and others at Vineyard Haven just about the end of the last war. He attempted to sail her east alone and got her as far as Gloucester before his legs gave out on him. Before arriving at Gloucester, he had put into Boston where an antisubmarine patrol was being maintained. According to reports, Parker went booming up the channel in the *Wentworth* with a magnificent disregard for the frantic signals from the patrol vessels of the Navy and Coast Guard. He hove to only when he reached an anchorage that suited him.

After reaching Gloucester, he lay tied up for some time, hobbling around and hoping his legs would regain their strength. They did not, however, and at last he gave up and called upon Freeman Closson, an old friend, for assistance. They sailed the old schooner to Maine, but Parker's active career was at an end and he had to retire ashore. He died not too long afterward. I believe his "official" age when he died was eighty-six, but there were some who believed he was much older.

He was a rugged individualist who had liked nothing better

59. The old *William C. Pendleton,* built as a sloop at Westerly, Rhode Island, as far back as 1857. Parker Hall took her off the mud in Pulpit Harbor where she had lain for years and put her to work again. Author's collection.

than to violate every ancient superstition of the seafaring profession. Blue paint he used in profusion, hatch covers flipped over on their backs, and he whistled, stuck knives in masts, and otherwise flouted seagoing convention with complete abandon. I asked him once how he managed to set a mainsail on those larger schooners with no hoisting engine and he replied, "C-c-c-cal'late I w-w-was j-j-jest a m-m-m-mite hef-hef-heftier than th' m-m-mains'l." He must have been nearing sixty or more at the time but he had the strength and agility of a much younger man. He was not tall, perhaps 5 feet 8 inches or even a little less, but he was so wide shouldered that he almost had to turn sideways to go through an average door, and he always did so going down a companionway. He probably weighed well over 200 pounds but it was mostly bone and muscle. In his old age, he had a fringe of white hair surrounding his bald dome and with his broad figure and round face he bore a faint resemblance to a cherubic but powerful kewpie doll.

One of the most likeable skippers on the coast was Fred Hutchins of Orland, owner and master of the *Fannie F. Hall* and later, the *Ella Clifton.* No one ever called him anything but "Cap'n Fred," and there seemed to be hardly a man or boy on the coast who didn't know and like him. Humorous and excitable, he laughed at the world from a pair of twinkling dark eyes below a thatch of iron gray hair. A naturally dark skin, tanned to the hue of cordovan leather, and a bushy mustache gave him the appearance of a benevolent walrus and his actions never belied his looks. He would do a favor for anyone and was a favorite for youngsters to go with. His wife accompanied him much of the time and their old schooners were home to a succession of boys from various parts of the coast.

When I knew him best, a lad named Mike Sullivan was with him and had become almost like a son to Fred and his wife. Mike had been raised in the tough South End of Boston, but some seafaring strain in his blood — inherited perhaps from a Galway fisherman ancestor — kept him hanging around the wharves when the lumber schooners were discharging. He was an agreeable lad and Cap'n Fred took a liking to him, arranging to take Mike with him for a trip or two in the *Ella Clifton.* The "trip or two" became a way of life for the boy and he stayed with the old man as long as he owned the vessel. Mike loved fun and a good time and was liked by everyone. He was also endowed with sea sense and was as capable a hand as though he had been born on the coast.

Cap'n Fred was a tough old rooster, and when in his sixties, survived a fall from his mainmast head, sustaining only a few broken ribs and a bruised jaw. After a restless week or so in the marine hospital, he emerged rugged as ever, to sail his schooner back east.

He finally retired to his home in Orland after spending over sixty years on the coast. When I last saw him, he was pitching wood into his barn, keeping well ahead of the two young fellows who were unloading the truck in the barnyard. He was in his late eighties and was possessed of all the vitality he had ever had.

It was told of him that he had never been to the westward of Cape Cod, and while I am inclined to doubt this, it could have been true. Certainly most of his life had been spent "Boston coastin'," as the phrase went and no one knew the coast from Cape Cod to Calais better than he. It was a standing joke that he hadn't looked at the chart for fifty years, and time and again I have heard him asked for a particular course and listened to him rattle off a complete set of sailing directions like a talking coast pilot. He was a mine of information about down-east loading ports and could always come up with detailed information as to the best berth, depth of water, and the courses in and out.

One old skipper who shall remain nameless for obvious reasons was noted for his interest in members of the opposite sex. He made very little money in his old schooner but what he did get on freights was mostly spent on various and sundry "daughters of joy." No sooner would he tie up to a wharf in Lynn or Boston, than he would get dressed in his best, a suit of greenish-black, and with his white hair and mustache "touched up" (some insisted with shoe blacking) set off uptown in search of feminine companionship. Sailors have never been noted for selectivity in "matters of the heart," but he exercised none whatsoever. Coastermen in more or less frequent contact with city life did not live a particularly austere existence, but this skipper was the champion of them all in the matter of persistence. What he spent on these "nymphs" no one knew, but having seen one or two of his companions, I can safely state it couldn't possibly have been worth it.

Arthur Stevens, my old man in the *Alice S. Wentworth,* was quite different from the other skippers I knew. Although capable as a seaman and coastal pilot, he never seemed to be really interested and his mind always seemed to be centered on affairs ashore. It may have been because of some particular situation at home, but although I was with him longer than with any other master, I never got to know him really well. He was not at all hard to get along with and was generous and good-hearted, but he seemed to live in a separate world of his own. I don't remember that he ever found fault with anything aboard the vessel in the time I knew him, but he would sometimes go for days without saying a word other than what was absolutely necessary. At times, however, he could talk interestingly and I have heard him in Billy Sawyer's store at Boothbay or visiting aboard some other schooner, holding forth with the best of them.

I will always remember Captain Ed Harper of the *Bloomer* for the way he loved to sail his homely old packet. Bluff-bowed and square-sterned, the old vessel nevertheless had a tall rig and Cap'n Ed made the most of it. He was one of the few coasting skippers I ever knew who seemed to love to sail for the sheer fun of it. Whether in company with other vessels or not, the old *Bloomer* always seemed to be under a press of canvas with more "glad rags" hung to the breeze than a mackerel schooner racing for Fulton Market. Cap'n Ed and his son Austin were fun to be with, and although I made only one short trip in the *Bloomer,* I remember her and her master and mate with pleasure.

Ben Paschal, of the stone schooner *Ervin J. Luce,* also liked to sail but principally because he was a natural driver. Nervous and intense, he was fearless and kept his old schooner moving for all she was worth. He never let a fair wind go by and never hesitated to start out in a foul one if he thought there was the slightest chance of getting anywhere. Once loaded, he took his schooner out if he could make it and kept her going if there was even half a chance along. He and Gene Webster of the *George R. Bradford* were great rivals. Both vessels were owned by the same company and they frequently sailed together, loading and discharging at the same ports. Paschal usually managed to get in first, much to Webster's disgust.

When Johnny Duke had the old *Emma* working in leisurely fashion around Penobscot Bay, he was pleasant, easygoing, and universally liked, but after he took over the *Annie & Reuben,* he was still pleasant and popular with others on the coast but he became a driver of the first order. He and the *Annie & Reuben* became known all along the coast, almost a legend in their own time. When the schooner was sold during the last war, Duke took over the power lighter *Progress,* formerly a sailing schooner and one of the later vessels built on Deer Isle.

George Robbins also had something of a reputation as a hustler in getting a vessel around, but when I was with him in the *Gilbert Stancliff,* he was not likely to press her too hard as she was showing her age and would not stand too much driving. In disposition he was rather uncommunicative and lacking in humor.

For Sant Lloyd I had a special liking. He got to be a good friend of my father's and undertook to stand *in loco parentis* when I was with him in the *Alice S. Wentworth* and the *Eugenie.* He kept me out of serious trouble and taught me a lot. He was ideal as a shipmate and his memory will always remain fresh in my mind. I lost track of him for several years, and some twenty years later, when I was able to track him down in his home town of Boothbay, I arrived a couple of days after his funeral. He had died of pneumonia.

13 | WEATHER

COASTERMEN live by the weather, and whatever else may be said, there is at least plenty of it along the New England coast. All kinds of jokes (most of them bad) have been made about Maine weather. One story is to the effect there are only two seasons in Maine — July and winter. Another libels the state as the second largest fog factory in the western hemisphere, only one degree better than the Bay of Fundy. I suppose there must be weather bureau statistics to refute these canards, but I am too lazy to look them up and I wouldn't believe them anyway if they lent any support to such monstrous exaggeration. I prefer to believe the evidence of my own experience. After some seven years off and on along the coast and uncounted time spent there before and since, I deny that Maine coast weather is that much worse than elsewhere in New England and maintain that one good day on the Maine coast is worth a dozen anywhere else.

There may be a little more fog than there is south of Cape Cod but there is also more wind and far better sailing weather. How the Maine coasting skippers used to curse the hot, breathless calms of Long Island Sound! During the summer in Maine (which, contrary to libelous reports, does include June, July and August and some beautiful sailing weather in September and October) there is often light fog or heavy haze in the mornings but this usually "scales up" before noon. Many yachtsmen seem to dread it and will lie at anchor, waiting for it to clear. It seldom bothered coasting skippers, however, and rarely prevented a vessel from sailing unless it developed into a real "fog mull."

Down east there are several degrees of fogginess. The lightest was generally designated as "a mite thick." Beyond that, it was "thick o' fog," "a dungeon o' fog," or even "a thick dungeon o' fog." When it reached the last stage, even the coasters hung to their anchors, and if it shut in on them while under way, they usually groped their way in to the nearest anchorage.

Once in a while there would be a heavy "fog mull" that could last for several days. It is probably these spells of heavy fog that give the coast its exaggerated reputation, but they happen with much less frequency than is popularly supposed. On such occasions, one lives in a world almost completely still. Sounds from shore or other vessels in the harbor are muffled and it is like existing in a void. Hours pass with only the faint whimpering of the gulls to be heard and the measured dripping of the moisture that forms in heavy drops under the booms and along every rope and spar.

Lying in a harbor where there was much steamboat traffic, anchor watches were necessary, and while the prescribed rules for fog signals at anchor were not always faithfully followed, it was desirable to keep one man on deck to beat the bell if there was any suggestion of the approach of a steamer or another sailing vessel.

We had a close call in the *Lulu W. Eppes* while anchored in Rockland one trip. We had finished discharging a cargo of box-boards at the Maine Central pier and had sailed at once, hoping to get across the bay and into Fox Island Thoroughfare before the fog, which could plainly be seen offshore, rolled in to the mainland. However, we just barely cleared the breakwater before it shut down on us, thicker than the proverbial pea soup. Around we came and headed back inside bound for the anchorage further up toward the north end. We lost sight of the breakwater almost at once and could only guess which way we were heading by the sound of the fog signal over our stern. Not wanting to get on to the mudflats too close to shore, the skipper let the *Eppes* run off a little and after taking a couple of soundings with the lead, decided we were in a good spot and anchored. Although we did not know it at the time, we were not too far off Tillson's Wharf and when the Bangor boat came groping in for her Rockland stop, she came perilously close to running us down. We heard her through the fog and I began a frenzied clanging of the bell. Still they came on, apparently unable to hear it above the noises of engines and their own signals. We also had the big Lothrop foghorn out and when we got the first glimpse of the towering stem headed almost for us, we really put our hearts into it and made the welkin ring with horn blasts, bell, and voices. They heard us just in time and sheered off with hooting whistle and jangling engine room bells ringing "full speed astern!"

In a more remote harbor or cove there is something even pleasant in this kind of fog. Perhaps not to the skipper chafing at the delay which prevents him from getting to his next loading or discharging port, although most of them had been too long on the coast to take it other than philosophically. There is nothing to do under such circumstances except eat and sleep, read or work on hobbies, and there is genuine peace and quietude, completely insulated from the rest of the world. How many times at the end of a period of frenzied business activity in the city in recent years have I wished I could be in one of my old bunks, waiting out a fog mull in some quiet down-east harbor!

Most of the coaster captains were excellent pilots as well they might be, having spent a lifetime along the coast until they were as familiar with it as their own back dooryards — sometimes, even more so. They seemed to find their way almost by instinct much as some of the old barnstorming plane pilots used to fly "by the seat of their pants." I have sailed countless miles through fog without ever seeing a recognizable landmark and without being given a worked-out course to steer by.

The old man would stand by the wheel and say, "Now let her go off a mite . . . that's fine, steady her there . . . what d'she say now?"

The reply might be " 'Bout west b' south, Cap'n."

"All right," he'd say, "keep her so for a spell."

On we would glide through the gray and hazy world of water until at last the skipper would speak up again. "Keep her off a mite more now . . . 'bout sou'west . . . that ought to fetch us into the bell . . . " and sure enough, it would, right on the end of the bowsprit.

Fog was not dreaded half as much as snow, for the wind during foggy weather was likely to be light, while in winter with a storm making up there was more wind than was wanted and it was nearly impossible at times to pick up signals from shore or other vessels unless they were right dead to windward. Running for shelter in a heavy snowstorm was an anxious time for all hands and contributed to more than one skipper's white hairs.

Most of the masters were weatherwise, however, and were seldom caught off guard. They had to rely on a barometer and their own observations for it was before the days of radios and weather broadcasts. "Red sky in the mornin' "; the wind "backin' " in and many other signs and portents made up the weather lore that enabled the coasting skipper to do his own forecasting. At night when the sky "gle'ned up" along the horizon, that was the quarter from which the wind might be expected the next day. Many old timers professed reliance on pet corns or certain twinges of rheumatism. Prevailing winds along the Maine coast in the summer are likely to be southwest, light in the early morning and increasing as the day wears on, dying out again at night. It is good weather for an eastbound passage but foul for getting up to the westward.

There are occasional westerlies and nor'westers, and these, too, are more than likely to go down with the sun. Once in a while there will be a "dry" easterly and then there is a real chance along. There is weight in the wind and it usually blows true and steady — unlike the fickle westerlies that can result in all kinds of stray "williwaws" and puffs under the land and at times "fush out" altogether. A southeasterly wind usually means rain or squally weather but some good passages can be made if it doesn't breeze on too strongly.

During the winter, the prevailing wind is just opposite to that which blows in the summer. Mostly, it settles in the easterly or northeasterly quadrant and blows hard, frequently with snow. Winter westerlies provide better sailing but they are bitterly cold at times and vessels tend to ice up fast from freezing spray. Wheel watches are short at such times, and a big pot of scalding black coffee is usually lashed on the stove.

There are some days in winter when there is marvelous sailing, especially "coming up through the land," sailing through the reaches and thoroughfares. Then the sky is a coldly perfect azure and the water darkly blue except where the wave crests are touched to brilliance by the sun. The reddish-brown of the rocks is half covered by ice and snow and the evergreens are black above them. The days are short but as long as the storms hold off, there are some wonderful passages to be made.

In any discussion of weather down east, one very noticeable feature is the way of speaking about points of the compass. North is "no'th," the "o" being long and the "th" almost hard. Northward becomes "Nor'ard." Reaching to the east, it is "No'theast" but toward the west, it becomes "Nor'west." Movies, radio, television and books conspire to have their seafaring men say "Nor'-east" and perhaps they do elsewhere, but seldom on the Maine coast.

On the opposite side of the compass, south is pronounced as it is written except there is the same hardness in the "th." The direction is "S'uthard." Toward the west it is "Sou'west" and to the east, "S'utheast," the "S'u" being pronounced as in "supply." There is no "Sou'east."

Courses were always given on compass points and the helm was "port" or "starboard." In emergencies it was "hard up" or "hard down." A course might be given such as "Let her go 'bout s'utheast b' south," "nothin' to" or "nothin' off" as the case might be.

I remember hearing of the indignation and dismay of one old skipper whose son returned from a hitch in the Navy where he had been a quartermaster. This was at the time when steering by degrees was being introduced and orders were given for "right rudder" and "left rudder." The boy attempted, deliberately or otherwise, to bring the Navy terminology home with him and the resulting explosion was volcanic. The old skipper fairly frothed at the mouth, according to a relative who witnessed the unhappy scene, and although peace was eventually restored with the son's reversion to the ways of his forebears, the old man always thereafter regarded Uncle Sam's Navy with contempt and disapprobation.

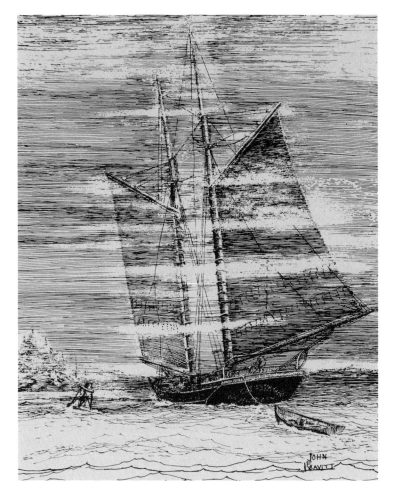

60. "A mite thick but thar's the bell!"

14 | PORTS OF CALL

Boxboards, unlike most square-edged or building lumber, were loaded anywhere a vessel could be tied up. If they were cut up-country they had to be teamed to places like Wiscasset, Damariscotta, Waldoboro, and other towns that were usually a few miles up-river from the coast. This often meant long tows with the yawl-boat and, incidentally, some magnificent scenery. The shores of nearly all the Maine coastal rivers are heavily wooded and the dark green of the trees above the reddish-brown of the ledges is unbroken for miles except occasionally by little clearings where a white house gleams against the dark background.

In some cases a lumber operator would set up a portable mill in the middle of a stand of timber near the bank of some river or "gunkhole" and build a temporary wharf of poles. Such places were Back River, Pemaquid, and several coves along the Muscle Ridge Channel. Dyer's Bay, Lincolnville Beach, Sargentville and a dozen other remote little harbors or loading wharves around Frenchman's Bay and along the coast east of Schoodic were familiar to the crews of all boxboard schooners.

The smaller bay coasters carrying cordwood, kiln wood, and, later, pulpwood, loaded in even more obscure places such as the outer islands along the coast and in the little inlets where the lines were made fast to the trees along the bank.

Bangor had long since ceased to ship the cargoes of lumber that once went down river by the millions of feet, but Calais took its place to some extent although the heyday of the lumber trade was really over. Staves were shipped in some quantity from Ellsworth and a few other places in the Mt. Desert area, but this business was coming to a close in the twenties.

Granite was shipped from Crotch Island in Deer Isle Thoroughfare, Hall's Quarry on Somes' Sound, St. George, Sullivan and various other places, several of them islands. Most of the stone in later years was granite block, used chiefly for cornerstones and similar heavy construction. Some of the schooners loaded paving blocks and smaller broken stone known as "grout," which had various uses. The increasing use of cement in building construction spelled the end of the stone trade, except for small shipments for special purposes.

As long as the lime trade endured, most of it was shipped from Rockland where the largest kilns were located in the later years. Thomaston had once held the lead in lime production and

Rockport had also produced large quantities to be shipped out in scores of vessels. In *Walden,* Thoreau speaks of a train headed up country, some of its cars loaded with Thomaston lime, and in the days when lime was all wood burned, it was considered to be the best quality obtainable. The Georges River leading up to Thomaston was a watery highway for hundreds of schooners bringing thousands of cords of kiln wood to feed the kiln fires. Any old vessel too poor to engage in any other trade could always eke out a living carting kiln wood to meet the insatiable demand.

Even today, riding over some of the back roads that touch tidewater in remote places, the remains of old crib wharves can still be seen. At these, schooner after schooner squatted in the mud while cords of wood were piled high on her decks. It took long experience and judgement to know the maximum cargo that could be taken aboard and allow the vessel to float free when the tide came. In the areas around the Brooksvilles, South Penobscot and other similar places, remains of these old wharves can be seen in almost every inlet.

At South Penobscot also can be seen the remains of Curt Durgain's brick kiln. The fires went out under the kilns in the twenties, but until then schooners standing up or down the narrow, twisting Bagaduce River were a common sight. At one time there were several other kilns in operation in the general area between the Penobscot River and Union River Bay for there was a good supply of clay for brick and pottery. A nationally famous pottery is still in operation at Bluehill today.

Far down the coast, around Red Beach particularly, schooners used to load plaster rock (gypsum, it is now called) but here,

too, the barges took over and the schooners vanished from the scene.

In the years before the first war, ice was a common cargo for schooners bound to southern ports, although few of the smaller two-masters engaged in the trade. Some of the three-masters would take ice south and come home with hard pine from Jacksonville and other Florida and Georgia ports. Ice came from Boothbay, Clark's Cove on the Damariscotta River, and dozens of other loading wharves in various areas. The old wharves can be seen at Clark's Cove today, and not too many years ago marine traffic on the river was heavy with vessels coming and going. In earlier days, larger, deep water ships loaded at Hampden and other places on the Penobscot River for the West Indies, South America, and even the Far East.

Of all the loading ports I knew on the Maine coast, Somesville was one of the pleasantest. The village was simply a collection of houses strung out along a mile or so of road that ran from Mt. Desert Bridge to Southwest Harbor, roughly parallel to Somes' Sound. The sound comes to a head at Somesville in the "pool" which forms a landlocked harbor a few hundred yards from the village. The Sound is a natural fjord cutting deep into the heart of Mt. Desert Island, extending several miles up from the sea. The mountains rise so high on either hand that only in the middle of the day does the sun strike directly down on the water, which is deep, dark and cold. A large coaster beating up the sound could, in many places, stand in until her jibboom was over the land before it was necessary to tack.

There is only one real landing place on the way up from the

61. Coasters anchored in Boothbay Harbor in the twenties. Author's collection.

62. Waiting at Portland for a fair breeze. Author's
collection.

sea: a wharf at Hall's Quarry, well up toward Somesville on the westerly side of the sound. Here, vessels loaded granite for New York and other points to the westward. Not far off the wharf the water is so deep that the big schooner *Delhi,* deep-loaded with granite, opened up and sank in minutes, her topmasts disappearing far below the surface.

A short distance up from the quarry wharf, the sound narrows to a bottleneck before opening into the pool. On an ebb tide it was a difficult place to enter and even with a fair wind, a yawl-boat was used to negotiate the narrows. Once through, however, there was a good anchorage in the middle of the pool, and if there was room at the sawmill wharf there was no need to anchor. Schooners grounded out at low water but it was soft mud around the shore and no damage was done. Some of the older and more leaky vessels took advantage of the situation to tighten their seams, using sawdust as caulking material. Bags of sawdust were taken from the huge pile at the side of the mill and dumped out on the mudflats around the vessel as she lay high and dry. When the tide made, the sawdust was sucked into the seams where, swelling with the water, it made the vessel tight as the proverbial bottle until she went to sea and lost it from the working of the hull in a seaway.

Sometimes even this measure proved ineffective, and at least one old schooner, the *Catherine,* had to be abandoned there at the age of over ninety years.

Somesville's social life consisted mainly of visits to the three principal stores in the early evening, one after the other. Two of them were owned by members of the Fernald family and the name of the third storekeeper I have forgotten. All were the old-fashioned type of country store where one might buy anything from hardtack to harrows. In cold weather the big stoves were fired up and around them were grouped the chairs of the "regulars," while more transient callers found seating space or support on or against boxes or barrels from which were dispensed sugar, flour, crackers and a dozen other sundries.

Here the crews of coasters were always welcome, especially in the spring. Few of the local people had been far away from town during the winter, radios were unknown, and although newspapers came in by mail, new faces were always welcome. There were the customary church suppers and similar social events, and when the dirt roads were passable, Saturday night usually found a dance in progress at Town Hill, a small community a few miles away on the road leading off the island.

In the spring, smelts could be had for the taking in the brooks emptying into the pool. A crocus sack tacked to a barrel hoop made a good dipnet, and a few scoops brought up enough fish to feed all the schooner crews in port.

By March the pool was sufficiently ice free to make it possible for schooners to get to the mill, and people were glad to see them come. The younger men in the crews found kindred spirits ashore, for after a long cold winter the young villagers of both sexes were like a bunch of colts let out to pasture. Spring was a very pleasant time to be in a Maine coast town.

I remember hauling into one remote little coastal village to load in early April when, under the spell of spring sunshine, a spontaneous party was launched that carried on spasmodically for three days. The weather that year had been cold and damp and the snow still lay in the shady places while the roads were rivers of half frozen mud. Suddenly, the day after we came in to load, the sun broke through the overcast and one could almost see things begin to come to life. On the lee side of the wharf house it was almost warm and long-chilled bones seemed to thaw out as if by magic. The process was assisted somewhat by a jug of potent applejack brought back by one of the dock workers when he returned from dinner. By the time it had gone the rounds a couple of times, the world began to look even rosier. Ideas were generated and before long the plan of promoting a dance at the grange hall spread like wildfire. Since no country dance was complete without a supper first, some of the women uptown got together and by quitting time a real party was shaping up.

Somehow, the word had spread around the countryside to some extent and there was a good crowd on hand. Those who have eaten an old-fashioned grange supper can imagine the quantities of buttermilk biscuit, dumpling stew, chicken and pies that were consumed and how they were enjoyed, particularly by those whose appetites had been whetted by a nip or two from the cider jug. After supper the tables were cleared and to the music of fiddle and piano the dance got under way. "Lady of the Lake," "Portland Fancy," and quadrilles followed each other in quick succession as the party gathered momentum. At three o'clock in the morning some of the hardier spirits were still carrying on although the piano player, a schoolteacher, had long since left. The fiddler was game, however, and quavering renditions of "Turkey in the Straw" and "Golden Slippers" sufficed to set the beat for more quadrilles and reels.

One night was enough for the soberer members of the community, but some of the younger crowd kept the party going for the next two evenings, far into the nights. My recollections of it are kaleidoscopic — food, drink, music, laughing girls, and blank spots that must have been snatches of sleep. To this day, I don't quite know what happened except that it was a spring revel of truly magnificent proportions.

Boothbay Harbor was by far the favorite harbor of refuge for coasters of all sizes. The holding ground was good, it was well protected and had well-marked entrances from either direction. Although the entire town was hospitable to coaster crews, Billy Sawyer's store on the waterfront was the favorite gathering place for masters, mates, and crews. It was both a clearinghouse of information on the whereabouts of vessels and crews and a ship chandlery where one might procure anything from a cabin lamp to a 2-ton anchor. The front of the store was stocked with coils of rope and gear of all kinds, while in the huge back room could be found second-hand equipment of every conceivable nature. Billy had been wrecking master for the district as had his father before him, and could supply blocks, chain, wheels, mast hoops, windlasses, and even a figurehead if need be. During the First World War there was a building boom at Boothbay and a number of large vessels were built, the last one being the four-master, *Josiah B. Chase,* launched in 1921. Few of these big schooners were operated regularly and many returned to Boothbay to lay

63. Bucks Harbor (South Brooksville), Maine, from the bluff overlooking the spring. Photo by Morris Chatto in the author's collection.

64. The "north end" of Rockland. Three-masted schooner *Willie L. Maxwell* in left foreground; stone sloops; and to the right, "a Johnny wood bo't." Author's collection.

up, awaiting better times. A few were sold and others came out of retirement but in those later years, Mill Cove was always a refuge for the big unemployed schooners, and some of them died there.

Around the Penobscot Bay region some of the best anchorages for refuge were in Fox Island Thoroughfare or the harbors and coves along Eggemoggin Reach. Vessels bound east out of Penobscot Bay or coming from the eastward to Rockland, Rockport, or Camden only, usually went through Fox Island or Deer Isle Thoroughfares but otherwise, the reach was generally preferred. After coming west over Bass Harbor Bar, Casco Passage and York Narrows required close pilotage and if there was any sign of fog, the wise coasting skipper usually headed for the Reach. There, the weather often remained clear while the fog lay over the western passages like a blanket of cotton wool. Bound east, Bass Harbor, Southwest Harbor, and Northeast Harbor offered good refuge, the first and second being preferred by coasters although yachtsmen have long preferred the third.

Coasters working through the Reach or around the head of the bay always looked on South Brooksville, more commonly called "Buck's Harbor," as a favorite anchoring place. There were several good reasons for this. The harbor is formed by a deep indentation in high land and lies directly behind an island which affords good protection yet leaves a wide deep channel in or out around both sides of the island. Situated at the westerly end of Eggemoggin Reach, it was a handy place for a schooner to duck in, either for overnight or a spell of bad weather. It has also been a favorite harbor in which to lay vessels up for the winter since ice seldom formed, due to the flow of the current around the island.

More than just its protection, Bucks Harbor was noted for its wonderful spring, piped down from the high bluff at the easterly side of the harbor. The pipe led down to the water's edge and it was an ideal place for coasters to take on water. They carried their water in wooden barrels, usually set on chocks just forward of the after house. They were set on their sides with a square hole cut in the top large enough to admit a dipper. Over the hole was tacked a canvas flap with an old pump bolt sewed into the edge to hold it down. Naturally the water had a tendency to collect dust, chips and other foreign matter and after a while to get pretty stale, but since it either had to be bought from waterboats at what was considered to be a high price or lugged aboard two buckets at a time at some loading or discharging port, it was not readily dumped out.

In Buck's Harbor, however, it was a comparatively simple job to take the empty barrels ashore in the yawl-boat at the right stage of the tide and simply lift the loose end of the pipe and let the water run them full. Back alongside the schooner, a whip was rigged to hoist them back aboard and drop them into their chocks. In other places, I have walked miles filling the barrels from the nearest well or pump, two pails at a time. The number of pails per barrel that it took was unbelievable.

Some of the larger cities like Portland, Rockland, Belfast, and Bangor were equally well known to coastermen and each had its own reputation.

Portland was an excellent harbor in which to lie for there were several good anchorages: Peak's Island Roads for those vessels in only overnight or whose skippers wanted to keep their crews from "paintin' the town" along Fore Street, and behind the breakwater under the South Portland shore for those more socially inclined. Some of the larger schooners used to anchor in the middle of the harbor under Munjoy Hill, the famous Eastern Promenade, and it was here that the big six-master *Edward J. Lawrence* furnished a flaming spectacle in the late twenties when she burned at her anchors. Most coasting skippers, however, believed the superstition that entering Portland for refuge was supposed to result in a stay of ten days at least. Also, it was a long way in and out for an overnight stop.

Rockland was protected by its long breakwater although the wide expanse of harbor was raked severely by easterlies. It was a favorite place for old vessels to "mud up," the flats at the north end being comprised of a particularly viscous type of mud. Rockland was also noted among coastermen for another reason altogether. Those inclined to romance of the "boughten" variety seldom had difficulty in finding what they sought at Rockland "Point," where a number of establishments flourished despite the more respectable elements of the city's society. This business declined with the coasting trade, although during World War II it made a "sidewalk comeback" when the shipyards flourished and payrolls grew large once more. During and just after the First World War there was a dance hall at the north end that was a famous haunt of coasting crews and their "lights of love"; it rejoiced in the unofficial name of "The Hog Rassel." It was no place for sedate social entertainment but every so often it was the scene of a memorable brawl.

Belfast was just an overgrown small town, having declined substantially as a shipping center in the years which marked the twilight of the sailing fleets. It was a good harbor, however, and there always seemed to be one or two small coasters loading or discharging cargo at one or the other of its deteriorating wharves.

Bangor, by the time World War I had ended, bore little resemblance to the rip-roaring city it had been a quarter century before in the days of the timber drives and at the height of the lumber trade, when thousands of schooners and other craft found their way up and down the river. No more did six or eight schooners "raft up" together to be towed down river by puffing tugs. Of the few vessels that navigated the reaches of the river in the later years most of them carried pulpwood to the mills at Brewer and sailed down the river with clean-swept holds.

Cape Porpoise, lying approximately halfway between Portland and the next good anchorage at Kittery (or Portsmouth) was a refuge of sorts but after one particular winter, coasters usually fought shy of it. Once inside, it is almost completely landlocked and sheltered from any wind, but the entrance is narrow and girt with low-lying ledges that spelt sure death to any schooner unfortunate to land on them.

During the cold months of 1919–1920 the Cape Porpoise ledges proved to be a graveyard for three schooners. In November, 1919, the big two-master *A. F. Kindberg,* hailing from Portland, piled up on the outer ledges in a desperate effort to reach shelter through the narrow entrance. Little more than a month later, on New Year's Day, two little three-masters came to grief in the same narrow channel.

The *Charles H. Trickey,* a 284-tonner built at Bath in 1879, was bound to Lynn with a load of boxboards and had sailed from Portland the day before. Unfortunately, the wind came out of the

65. The ill-fated *Mary E. Olys* deep-loaded with stone. From the
Frank Wilson collection, courtesy Captain W. J. L. Parker.

northeast with thick snow when she was too far to the westward of Cape Elizabeth to beat back to the safety of the harbor she had just left. It grew worse so rapidly that the skipper decided not to try for Kittery but to attempt the narrow entrance of Cape Porpoise, which was right under his lee. With the visibility almost zero, he picked up the light on Goat Island but missed the spindle that lay just outside of it and piled up on the ledges at the top of the high water, about midnight. With the tide ebbing, there was less and less danger of the schooner breaking up and the crew, although anything but comfortable, remained where they were.

In the meantime, another little three-master, the *Mary E. Olys,* was struggling to the westward with a cargo of granite from Stonington for New York. Deep loaded as she was, she was like a half-tide ledge and how she had managed to survive as far as she did was something of a mystery. However, along toward morning, Captain Hatch decided he had enough and since he could not make Portland, he also decided to try for Cape Porpoise. He made his landfall perfectly but through the curtain of snow made out the spars of the *Charles H. Trickey* and bore off to avoid the same fate. He swung too far, however, and before he realized his mistake he was hard and fast on the other side of the channel with the tide still ebbing and his vessel badly holed. It was then about six o'clock in the morning.

At daylight the storm abated enough to get the crews of both schooners ashore and the revenue cutter *Ossipee,* stationed at Portland, was sent down to the scene of the wrecks. It was obvious she could do nothing toward getting the vessels off, however, for both were badly holed and showing signs of breaking up. The gale was of fairly short duration and the next day had died down sufficiently for salvage workers to begin stripping them of sails, gear, and equipment that had any value. Lighters took off the cargoes and these were forwarded in other vessels. The schooners broke up shortly afterwards and were gone by spring. From then on, few coasting skippers seemed willing to seek sanctuary at Cape Porpoise and would almost invariably run for Kittery instead.

15 | PACKETS AND BAY COASTERS

ALTHOUGH passenger traffic had long since turned to railroads, steamboats, and automobiles, freight for the coastal towns was still carried in schooners until well into the thirties. Supplies for the village stores in the form of grain, feed, farm machinery, sugar, flour, and a hundred and one sundries still reached the towns of eastern Maine in the holds of packet schooners. These little vessels sailed on more or less regular schedules from Widgery's wharf in Portland, often called the Portland packet pier. They ranged in size from 25 to 60 or 70 tons and most of them had been built, or rebuilt, with a "riz" deck to gain more under-deck cargo capacity.

Ask anyone familiar with the Portland waterfront during the early twenties for the names of some of the packets and one of the first he would be sure to mention would be the *Lizzie J. Clark* of Jonesport, owned and operated for many years by various members of the Peabody family of Beal's Island. Built at Pembroke, Maine, in 1867, the *Lizzie* became the Jonesport packet just before the First World War. Like most vessels in the trade, she was a "riz-decker," her poop being extended forward to the fore rigging, leaving a short well-deck for the windlass and anchor gear.

For many years she maintained an almost steamerlike schedule and at regular intervals could be found at Widgery's wharf taking aboard cargo of infinite variety to stock the shelves of Jonesport and Beal's Island stores. Like many other packet skippers, her masters made shopping trips uptown on occasion to make special purchases for women customers in the home ports. A book of dress patterns, yarn for knitting, sewing materials, and maybe a whole or partial new set of dishes often reached a far eastern town in the hold or cabin of a packet. Often it did not pay the village storekeeper to handle a single order for things not generally included in his regular stock of goods so the packet skipper was pressed into service as an errand boy.

In an earlier day, the more remote towns had been served by "traders," small vessels with a barnlike structure built between the masts and stocked with the gew-gaws that women like, as well as toys and other things appealing to the young, and Barlow knives, Red Jack boots, and such things for the fisherman husbands. George Wasson has written interestingly of this trade as it flourished when he was a boy on the coast in the eighties.

Many coastermen, particularly those with families ashore,

66. The *Lizzie J. Clark* — "bustin' it wide open." Courtesy John Quincy Adams.

liked the packet trade. They were never away for very long and there was always interest and excitement in Portland to make them forget the dull monotony of life in the little isolated towns along the coast. A few of them were regular patrons of the various establishments along Fore Street and its environs, where one could buy a few drinks and, if so inclined, secure the attentions of an undiscriminating inamorata.

Such nymphs were hardly "visions of delight" even to a hard-case and lusty coasterman, but they occasionally furnished relief from the work-hardened women left at home, and occasionally a girl latched on to one of the unmarried men in the crews. I know of one young skipper who fell head over heels for a girl in one of the better-known houses and married her. At first, it almost looked like one of those romances which could survive under any circumstances. The girl brought her belongings aboard the little schooner her new husband was sailing and, for a year or so, everything seemed to be idyllic. Eventually, however, the regular visits to the city seemed to renew old attractions, and there came a day when the wife climbed back on the wharf and announced she was going to stay over a trip in Portland. Her husband had the lines cast off, all but a last bight, and a fair wind was blowing. He argued with her as he hoisted the foresail. She remained adamant and when he gave her a last chance to get back aboard, she stamped her foot and swore she wouldn't move. "O.K.," he said, and yelled at the youngster who constituted the crew to cast off the last bight of line. The offshore breeze filled the sail and before the lady could change her mind (even if she had wanted to) the vessel was on the way home, her erstwhile husband making sail as they headed out toward Spring Point Light. That was the end of a marriage.

Another well-known packet running to some of the towns along the reach was the green-painted *E. T. Hamor,* a handsome little 52-ton schooner built on Mt. Desert Island in 1889. She had previously been owned in Mt. Desert Ferry, but in her last years hailed from Portland. At last, I believe, Fred Seavey at Bluehill bought her and hauled her up on the blocks with the intention of rebuilding her. She fell over, however, and was so badly damaged that she was stripped and abandoned, her spars and gear being used to equip the somewhat larger *Joanna Durgain* which was extensively rebuilt and renamed *Katie D. Seavey.* This was the third rebuilding for the same vessel and there were some grounds for believing it may have been the fourth.

The *Katie D. Seavey* had originally come to Penobscot Bay some time in the seventies as the schooner *Hudson.* She was supposed to have been built at Westbrook, Connecticut, in the fifties, but Captain Ed Harper — who remembered her well when she first arrived — told me once that she was even much older and was originally a Hudson River sloop, completely rebuilt at Westbrook and given new documentation. Certainly her hull had all the appearance of those vessels built and sailed up and down the Hudson. She had the typical "Hudson River sheer" and the apple bows so common in the sloops, many of which were rebuilt and rerigged for service elsewhere. In any case, she sailed as the *Hudson* until the eighties, when she was bought by the Grays at Brooksville; rebuilt and renamed *Letty M. Gray.* She was then listed in the ship register as the ex-*Hudson.* In 1902, after having

67. Island communities were often supplied by "traders" in the old days. They had just about disappeared by the time of the First World War, but George Wasson has written of them in his *Sailing Days on the Penobscot.* This drawing of the schooner *Sarah Elizabeth* riding out a southeaster at Isle au Haut was inspired by a drawing in one of his sketchbooks, now in the G.W. Blunt White Library at Mystic Seaport Museum.

68. The handsome little packet schooner *E.T. Hamor*.
Author's collection.

been through a very complete rebuilding, she was launched as the *Joanna Durgain,* having been deepened and given the "riz" deck common to so many packets. She still had most of her original rocker sheer and was a handsome vessel. Despite her bluff bows she was a very smart sailer, for she still had the big rig built into her on the sound where the light weather conditions that prevailed allowed the coasters to carry taller spars and bigger rigs than most down easters would put into their vessels. When I was in the *Alice Wentworth* we sailed from Southwest Harbor in company with the *Durgain,* and although the *Alice* was substantially larger, we had difficulty leaving the smaller vessel astern.

The final rebuilding job was done in the late twenties and was a rough one. Her original sheer was not restored and the shorter rig from the *E. T. Hamor* clipped her wings so she lost any pretensions to speed. She was one of the last packets in operation, however, and became a familiar fixture at Widgery's wharf. She was at last sold south at the outbreak of World War II, but on the way down got ashore on Cuttyhunk Island and left her timbers to whiten in the sand.

The *Lois M. Candage,* one of the last of the Camden dude cruisers, ran quite steadily to Lubec and other eastern ports in the later years of the packet trade. Unlike the majority of the packets which depended upon sails alone, she had an auxiliary engine installed in her stern, powerful enough to buck the currents which run fast in the Quoddy Bay area. Earlier, she had operated out of East Bluehill under sail with Freeman Closson as skipper. She was originally an older vessel which I believe was built up around Steuben in the seventies or eighties, but in 1912 she was so completely rebuilt by George Candage at East Bluehill that she received a new documentation and was named for his wife. Freeman Closson had her for about fifteen years in the packet trade and classified her as a comfortable and able little schooner but a dull sailer. After leaving the dude cruise fleet she was purchased by a restaurant in Damariscotta as a tourist attraction. Some superficial repairs were made and she stayed afloat for a time, but while being towed down to South Bristol for a winter tie-up, something happened to her and down she went to the bottom alongside the old steamboat wharf. After lying on bottom for most of one winter, she was raised and taken back to Damariscotta and grounded in the mud alongside the restaurant. At the time this is written, she is still on bottom, the tide coming and going in her aging hulk.

High on the list of packet schooners was the handsome little *Railroad*, built at Castine in 1872. With Ralph Merriam as skipper, she ran for several years to Nor'west Harbor and Oceanville on Deer Isle and also to Boothbay Harbor, where she was a familiar sight grounded out alongside Hume's Dock inside the footbridge. She was a shapely little schooner and may originally have been one of the "clipper" type of fishermen, many of which became coasters in their later years. She was never given the raised deck which so often spoiled the looks of packets. She had a lively sheer and a tall rig, and why Merriam left her to take over that homely marine monstrosity, the power freighter *B. B. W.*, no one could figure out. He was probably smarter than the rest for he must have decided the age of sail was at an end and a power vessel was the more practical if not the more aesthetic answer to the problem.

69. The bluff-bowed *Katie D. Seavey, ex-Joanna Durgain, ex-Lettie M. Gray, ex-Hudson*. Courtesy Roger C. Peterson.

In the early thirties the *Railroad* was laid up at Boothbay and was at last sold to some people who were reported to be taking her out to the South Seas for service as an island trader. Apparently they spent all their money on paint and neglected a few bad planks in the bottom. Sailing from Boothbay after her partial refit, she got only a short way to the westward before she opened up and sank, giving her crew barely time to get away in the yawl-boat.

Equally famous in later years was the former fisherman *William Keene.* Built at Damariscotta in 1866, she had for many years been one of the Grand Banks fishing fleet before her type became obsolete and she joined the coasting fleet. Captain Bill Butler, living at South Bristol in the 1950s at more than eighty years of age, made his first trip to the Banks in the *Keene* when he was only nine years old.

Like many other clipper fishermen of her type, she came at last to the coasting fleet and hauled cargoes of wood, coal, and brick around the coastal waters. Later, she was rebuilt and given a raised deck. Taking her place in the Portland packet fleet she soon became well known. Her skipper in later years was Captain Bert Webber, who always seemed to get the most out of her. She occasionally made a trip to Gloucester or Boston between regular runs down east and was often found at Shurtleff's wharf in Portland discharging salt from Gloucester.

As a fisherman she had been a handsome schooner but, when rebuilt, the raised deck and the high, boxy forward house installed to cover the hoisting engine, did nothing to improve her looks. Her long head had vanished, being replaced by a stubby knee head, and although she never became badly hogged, she was not a

thing of beauty. Nevertheless, she was a hard vessel to pass, and once her underbody had been seen hauled out on the ways, it was not difficult to understand why. Any vessel that did pass her had something to brag about. I was sailing as a guest in a large schooner yacht in Penobscot Bay in the late thirties when the *Keene* came up astern and passed us, much to the amazement of the yacht's owner but not to mine. When the last war broke out, the *Keene* was sold to a candy company which needed vessels of any kind to freight sugar from the West Indies or Cuba. She was rebuilt extensively, fitted with an auxiliary engine and started south to a new life. She was too old to learn a new trade, however, and did not last too long once she got there.

Another ex-fisherman, the *Lillian,* owned and skippered by Captain Bob Lash, ran quite regularly with cannery supplies and products between Friendship and Portland. She had power in her stern and a wheelhouse aft which made the winter runs a little more comfortable. When the coasting business came to an end she became a dude cruiser, operating first out of Camden and later out of Belfast where she finally died.

The *Annie F. Kimball,* also a dude cruiser in her last years, was a well-known packet and bay coaster operating out of Southwest Harbor and towns further east. She was a handsome little schooner of 41 tons built by Jacob Farnham at Linekin Bay in 1886. She had many of the characteristics of the fishing schooners of the period, but the newspapers of the day announced she was built for the coasting trade. For a time in her later years, she was equipped with a gasoline auxiliary engine, being then owned in Machias. She was one of the earlier vessels in Frank Swift's dude

70. The *Katie D. Seavey* at Widgery's wharf, Portland. Courtesy
Roger C. Peterson.

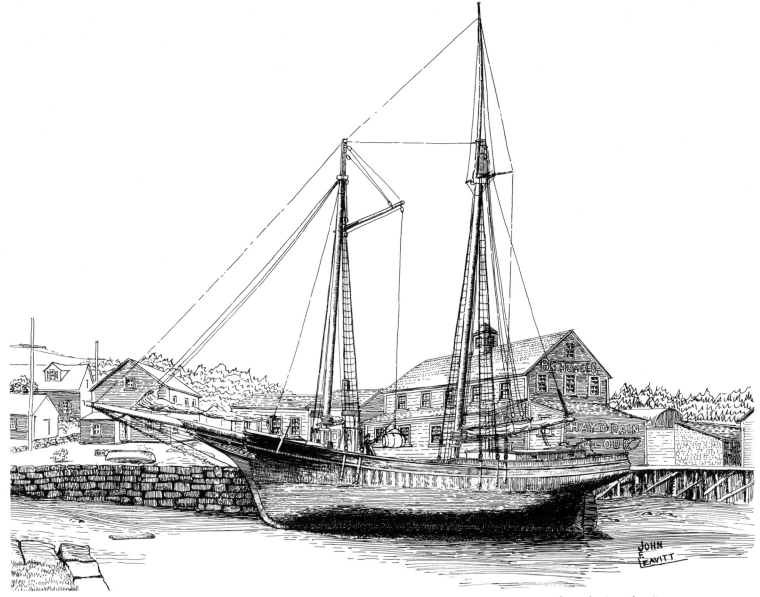

71. The *Railroad* at Hume's Dock, inside the footbridge at Boothbay Harbor, Maine. She grounded out at every low tide, affording the opportunity for a look at her handsomely shaped hull.

cruise fleet and she lasted until the Second World War, although in her last years, she became very limber, and some of those who sailed in her declared one could see her work when there was any sea running. She was at last hauled on to the mud behind the Camden Shipyard and there soon went to pieces.

The little *Hattie Loring* of 46 tons had been built in Gouldsboro in 1895 and ran for years as a Portland packet. She was later sold to Nova Scotia but came back in the late twenties as an auxiliary schooner, then as a power lighter, and was at last given a knockabout sailing rig, the engine still furnishing the principal motive power. She established a questionable claim to fame by appearing briefly in a moving picture made at Vinalhaven just after the war. Remembering the smart looking little packet that I used to know, I almost left the theater where the opus was being shown. All I could think of was a blowsy, female wino.

Several schooners were built at Deer Isle just before or after the First World War including the *Enterprise, Mercantile, Progress, Billings Brothers, Philosopher,* and the last working coaster to be built in the State of Maine, the *Endeavor.* Most of them operated as packets although like many other craft which survived to the end, they carried any cargoes available in later years. Built of soft woods, they had to be repaired and rebuilt several times but at least one of them may be still afloat.

The *Enterprise* and *Mercantile* became dude cruisers and the latter is still operating out of Camden while the former was burned only a few years ago. The *Progress* was still in operation as a power lighter with Captain Johnny Duke as master until after the

last war, and I have heard the *Philosopher* was operating in Costa Rican waters for several years after 1945.

The *Endeavor* was built at Little Deer Isle in 1938 by Captain Albert Shepard and was operated profitably for several years. She was launched with a raised deck and, although such features as turned stanchions for the fly rail and fancy mouldings and carvings were omitted, she was a neat and practical schooner carrying large cargoes for her size and being noted as a smart sailer. Like many vessels of her type she was built with a centerboard, but when she was sold to New York it was removed and some sort of fin keel substituted. Because she was new many cargoes were available that were denied to the aged and decrepit survivors of the old fleet, but eventually she, too, was reduced to carrying pulpwood like the rest. This caused Captain Shepard to sell her just before the outbreak of World War II.

For many years one of the smartest of the bay coasters was the handsome *Mildred May* of 54 tons, also owned by Curt Durgain and built in Brooksville in 1896. She was narrower of beam and taller sparred than most of her contemporaries and had the reputation of being a little "tender-sided," but she never seemed to get into serious trouble. Certainly she was fast for a coaster and Captain Ralph Leland was never content to let her idle along as long as the breeze held.

These bay coasters were of about the same size as the packet schooners but had no regular schedules and engaged in general freighting, mostly along the eastern coast and Penobscot Bay areas.

The little 37-ton *Mabel* was one of these. She was built as a centerboarder at Millbridge in the eighties and was one of the smaller vessels in the fleet. For many years she freighted brick, coal and cordwood around the bay, being owned for some time by Steve Branscom, a coal and wood dealer in Northeast Harbor. Freeman Closson went in her for him and it was aboard this little schooner that I renewed my acquaintanceship with Freeman and Bertha when cruising down east with friends in the thirties.

She was eventually sold to a chap named Walton in Lubec to become a power cannery lighter with only the foremast left standing and a pilothouse erected on top of the old after house. For a short time prior to that, she was apparently chartered by Frank Swift to become the first vessel he operated in the dude cruise business. Later, he bought her back again and restored a full schooner rig but after a year or two, sold her to private ownership to become a floating houseboat. An attempt to get her up to the westward was unsuccessful, and she went to the bottom off Seguin when her aged seams opened.

Another small schooner that ended her days as a dude cruiser was the little *Clinton* of only 22 tons, built at Millbridge in 1886. While coasting she was always owned east of Mt. Desert, her home port for many years being Machias. The amazing thing to me was the fact that so many of these vessels had been considered "run out" when I was a youngster on the coast fifteen to twenty years before.

One forlorn and broken down old bay coaster, the *Stephen Taber*, underwent a metamorphosis in 1936 when Captain Fred Wood of Orland bought her for a song, hauled her out on the blocks of the old McKay & Dix yard on Verona Island, and com-

pletely rebuilt her. She had been badly hogged, but he ruthlessly ripped away plank and timbers until she settled down on the blocks, her keel as straight as a gun barrel. Working carefully, he made an excellent job of it and, when finished, she was a handsome little vessel, almost as good looking as on the day she was launched at Glenwood Landing on Long Island Sound sixty-five years before. If she survives until 1971, she will have reached the century mark. Fred Wood operated her for several years in the pulpwood business, picking up his cargoes at various islands off the shore and carrying them to Bucksport, Brewer and Belfast until advancing years and poor health induced him to sell her to Captain F. B. Guild of Castine, who introduced her to the dude cruise business. He in turn sold her to Havilah Hawkins, also a cruise schooner operator. He kept her well and improved her appearance and equipment. After a few years, he sold her to build a new vessel, designed particularly for the cruise business which he named the *Mary Day*. The *Taber* continued in the same business under other ownership and has been operating out of Camden.

A once-familiar sight in the early twenties was the green-painted *Clara B. Kennard*, a 75-ton former Portsmouth bricker built at Weymouth, Massachusetts, in 1886 and engaged for many years in carrying brick from the kilns near Portsmouth, New Hampshire, to Boston or other ports where they were in demand. Some time after the turn of the century she was bought by Captain Phil Billings of Deer Isle and South Brooksville. In 1925 he sold her and had the 60-ton *Philosopher* built at Deer Isle in the same yard where the *Enterprise*, *Mercantile* and *Progress* had been launched. She was a raised deck schooner with a sheer like a

72. The seventy-year-old *William Keene* unloading a cargo of salt at Manset, Maine.

73. The *Endeavor* — last coaster built in the state of Maine, 1938 —
towing out of Bluehill with a load of pulpwood about 1939.

wooden shoe. As a yacht and ship broker, about 1937 I engineered the sale of her to a couple of young exmates in the United Fruit Company who took her to Costa Rica. When I first went down to see Captain Phil about selling her, he was then living at South Brooksville and he took me into the barn to show me the model from which she was supposed to have been built. Looking at the half model and recalling the actual appearance of the schooner, I noted a marked difference in the sheer. When I ventured a remark to that effect, Captain Phil drawled "Well, I cal'late 'tis some diff'rent. When they sot her up they must have riz her up jest a mite too fur aft." Remembering how the stern of the *Philosopher* swept upward like that of a Spanish galleon, this seemed to me to be a masterpiece of understatement.

Brooksville was where I first saw the *Lewis R. French,* lying behind the island with her decks blown apart. An explosion of some kind had torn her up pretty badly in the early twenties and for some time she lay neglected until she was purchased and rebuilt into a cannery lighter. She had been built as a fishing schooner or smack at South Bristol in 1871, and was a good-looking little schooner like most of those built by A. & M. Gamage. When rebuilt, however, she had only a plain stem and a big wheelhouse aft, and all semblance of good looks had vanished.

The tiniest schooner working in Penobscot Bay was the 14-ton *Mable C. Snow,* built in 1878 at Camden and owned for many years in North Haven. Her owner-skipper used to sail her around the bay single handed, picking up driftwood from the water and the shores of the uninhabited islands. When he had a full load he would take it to Rockland or Rockport and sell it for kiln wood or cordwood. In the earlier days, when the sawmills at Bangor and Brewer were operating at capacity, a steady stream of driftwood floated down the river and into the bay and a number of small vessels made a living picking it up.

Another pair of small vessels which seldom ventured out of the bay were the *C. Taylor 3rd.* and the *William C. Pendleton.* The former was built at Middletown, Connecticut, in 1853 and was bought to be brought down east in the late eighties.

The *Pendleton* had been built at Westerly, Rhode Island, in 1857 and was originally a sloop. She was rerigged prior to coming to Maine in the nineties. She was first owned in Boothbay, but later in the Penobscot Bay area. The *C. Taylor 3rd.* was owned in Union River Bay when she finally gave out about the time of the First World War and she was hauled up on the bank beside the Mt. Desert bridge and left to die.

The *Pendleton* in her later years freighted kilnwood and cordwood and coal out to the islands, but when her owner died, she was abandoned in Pulpit Harbor on North Haven Island. After lying on the mud with the tide ebbing and flowing through her hull for several years, she was hauled off by Captain Parker Hall and patched up for further use. He drove her gaping seams full of gump wedges, scrounged some old sails and gear, and before long had her afloat and working. I once asked him why he bothered with such an old wreck and he answered cheerfully in his usual stacatto fashion, "W-w-wa'nt n-n-nawthin' th' matter w-w-with her 'ceptin' sh-sh-she was j-jest a m-m-mite h-h-h-hollers-seamed."

In any case, he sold her after a while, probably turning a

profitable penny on the deal, and the last time I saw her was in the late thirties bound down the bay with a load of cordwood for Monhegan. We were bound up the bay in a big schooner yacht and just as we passed her, a squall struck down off the Camden Hills. For a few minutes we were so busy I didn't have a chance to look for the *Pendleton,* but when I did, she was still boiling down the bay although where her mainsail had been was a mass of rags and tatters. It had blown out like a piece of tissue paper.

Visitors to Vinalhaven in the early thirties saw on the bank the hulk of the little 29-ton *Ella Eudora,* built at Mt. Desert in 1871 for Captain Ed Harper, then living at Goose Cove. He ran her as a general bay coaster for several years and in the nineties sold her and bought the larger *Bloomer.* The *Ella Eudora* spent her last years running coal and wood for Charles Robertson, the fuel dealer at Vinalhaven, but she was finally abandoned on the west shore of Carver's Harbor.

Another seagoing matriarch which met her end in the same place was the schooner *Joyce Rebecca,* built in 1837 at New London, Connecticut, under the name of *Planter.* Originally a fisherman, she became a coaster in the nineties when she was sold to Waldoboro, Maine. Shortly after that she was extensively rebuilt and received the euphonious name which graced her for the rest of her life. Her career was a long one, for she was still hauling coal, I believe, at the age of ninety-nine years. About 1936, she was anchored in Carver's Harbor one stormy night with no one aboard. Next morning she was missing, and it was some time before someone discovered a mass of broken timber at the head of the harbor which was all that was left of the *Joyce Rebecca.* She had parted

her rusty anchor chain, driven ashore, and disintegrated like the "Deacon's wonderful one-horse shay."

Many of these old schooners were kept in operation for incredible lengths of time, but when they did "hit the beach," they fell apart completely. This happened to the old *Emma,* built at Stockton in 1871. While not so ancient as some, she had carried granite and other heavy cargoes for years and had been subjected to hard usage. Johnny Duke, later in the *Annie & Reuben,* used to go in her, but after his wife's death he gave up the old vessel. Captain Elmer Greenlaw, formerly in the *L. L. Hamlin,* was her last master, carrying cordwood and coal to the islands and even venturing a couple of trips to Boston with "edgings" to sell for firewood.

In the late thirties, with his mainsail blown out and being alone, Captain Greenlaw hired a lobster fisherman to tow him to Rockland from Vinalhaven. Working out through one of the passages, the *Emma* took a sheer and bounced on a ledge. It was enough to open her up, however, and the old man barely got into his yawl-boat before the schooner slid out from under him and sank out of sight.

Although she sailed a few trips with the boxboard fleet in her first years down east, the 58-ton *Mattie* — recently a dude cruiser at Camden — was better known as a bay coaster although she was not an infrequent visitor to Gloucester and Boston. Built in 1882 at Patchogue, Long Island, New York, as the *Grace Bailey,* she was bought by Captain H. L. Black of South Brooksville to replace the *Oakwoods,* accidentally rammed and sunk by a U.S. submarine near the Cape Cod canal just after the First World War.

74. The *Stephen Taber* with a cargo of pulpwood. Captain Fred Wood aft and his crew (Mrs. Wood) on the deckload amidships. Author's collection.

75. The *Emilie Belle* at Vinalhaven. Courtesy Murray G. Peterson.

When the *Mattie* came east she was touted as being a possible rival of the *Alice S. Wentworth* in the matter of sailing. She was a wide shoal centerboarder of about the same size and type as the *Wentworth,* but she was never quite so fast. When both vessels were running boxboards to Lynn, there were several opportunities to try them out, and the *Alice* always sailed away from her.

At one time there were two *Lillians* and two schooners named *Maude S.* The older *Lillian* was built at Belfast as a coaster in 1873, and the second vessel of the name was the little exfisherman, built at Boothbay in 1876. The two schooners named *Maude S.* (after the famous race horse) were both built in 1883, the smaller one of 45 tons at Millbridge, while the larger one of 75 tons was launched at Bath as a fisherman, later becoming a coaster and hailing from Machias.

Familiar to everyone in the Union River Bay area was the 69-ton *J. Chester Wood,* which "Skip" Mazrall took over after he left the *Storm Petrel.* In her later years it was said he used to take her over to Contention Cove in Surry and let her sink every fall. Next spring he would drive the plugs back in again, pump her out, clean her up, bend the sails, and be ready for business once more.

Another late survivor was the *Emilie Belle,* a 27-ton bay coaster built at Patchogue, New York, in 1868 and sold to Maine long before the First World War. She was a sad sight in her old age with a foremast that came from an even smaller schooner and looking as though the planking on her bluff bow was coming adrift from the stem. However, she managed to keep afloat until about 1940, when she settled to the bottom of Carver's Harbor and stayed there.

There were many others of course, the *Lydia M. Webster* — later a dude cruiser; the old North River bricker *William P. Boggs,* hardly more than a sailing lighter; and the *Ella,* which drifted down east in the thirties.

76. The *Mattie,* ex-*Grace Bailey,* still working as a "dude" cruiser out of Camden, Maine. Author's collection.

77. The *Annie & Reuben* ready to discharge cargo. John R. Herbert
photograph from Peabody Museum, Salem, Massachusetts.

16 | STONE DROGHERS

AMONG the vessels built or rigged for a special trade, the stone schooners were the most easily identified. In the later years, they had come to replace the big sloops that once handled all of the granite cargoes along the coast. These schooners invariably handled their own cargoes as the sloops had done. For a long time it was felt that only sloops were practical for the stone trade, for it was a rig that easily allowed a big derrick boom to be slung from the mast. Most of the sloops were built or owned at Chebeague Island in Casco Bay and worked as far south as Philadelphia and eastward to the Canadian line.

The schooners, with the exception of the *George R. Bradford* and the *Anna Sophia,* began life as general traders. When rebuilt for the stone trade, the mainmast was stepped as far aft as it could go with the result that enough room was left between the masts to allow a derrick boom to be rigged and swing clear. It resulted in a tremendous foresail that in some cases was almost bigger than the mainsail and, "winged out" with foresail to one side and mainsail to the other, most of the stone vessels could walk away from other vessels when the wind was dead aft.

At sea the long heavy derrick boom was lashed down on deck, but the wire falls with their steel blocks were left rove off and triced to the fore rigging. To handle such heavy gear, more power than could be furnished by the average gasoline hoisting engine was necessary. Therefore, most of the vessels had a steam-powered hoister with the boiler in the hold abreast of the foremast, the stack projecting upward through the deck, protected by a 3-foot coaming and heavy wooden hinged covers that folded down around the stack. It was not completely watertight, of course, but it prevented any large amount of water from getting below. Once alongside a wharf, ready to discharge, the wire falls were hooked to the head of the boom, and it was topped up with the heel in an oversized gooseneck fitting or sometimes resting in a hollow socket gouged out of heavy timber that was bolted to the deck at the foot of the foremast. The actual hoisting falls were also hooked into the bail of the boom, the hauling part also being led to the steam winch.

Most of the smaller schooners in later years loaded at Crotch Island, on the southwesterly side of Deer Isle Thoroughfare, and delivered their cargoes to Boston. Much stone was still shipped to New York from Hall's Quarry on Somes' Sound, St. George, and a few other quarry ports, but it was usually carried in the larger two- and three-masted schooners which were loaded and discharged by wharf derricks.

The smaller schooners on the Boston run were almost invariably loaded just shy of the sinking point. I have seen the *Annie & Reuben* with something over 200 tons of stone aboard, lying at Crotch Island wharf with the water flowing through the scuppers to the height of an inch or more on the main hatch coaming over the deck. This in a flat calm. Loaded in such fashion, the schooners resembled half-tide ledges when at sea, and it is sure the hatches were well battened down and the pumps going steadily the entire trip.

Of all the later stone fleet, the *Annie & Reuben* was one of the most noted. She was built at Bath in 1891 registering 128 tons, and during the early part of her career engaged in the general coasting trade. Later on, however, she was purchased by John L Goss & Co. on Deer Isle and refitted and rerigged for the stone trade. She was a powerful schooner and a good sailer and became an even better one after the change in rig. Winged out before the wind she was almost impossible to catch.

George Robbins had her for a while after leaving the *Mary E. Lynch,* and he, in turn, handed her over to Johnny Duke, destined to become her most famous skipper. Previously in the old *Emma* he had no great reputation as a driver, but when he took over the *Annie & Reuben,* he proceeded to astonish everyone. There wasn't a harbor between Deer Isle and Boston where she

wasn't known, although Captain Johnny never went in if there was half a chance along. Even in her old age he used to keep her moving.

For several years a legend persisted that when the *Annie & Reuben* came into Portland it meant rain, and the news of her arrival there was always noted in the daily waterfront column of the *Press Herald,* more space being devoted to the event than would have been given the arrival of some ocean liner.

During World War II she was finally sold to go south for the Cuban sugar trade but, like several others, she got ashore on one of the New Jersey beaches and never came off.

Other well-known stone droghers were the *Ervin J. Luce* and the *George R. Bradford,* owned by the Rockport Granite Company of Rockport, Massachusetts. In the later years, however, they operated between Maine quarry ports and Boston. John L. Goss & Co. owned two other vessels, the *Mary E. Lynch* and the *Mabel E. Goss,* both having been especially rerigged for the stone trade.

The *George R. Bradford* was built especially for the business in 1895 at Essex in the James yard, and was supposed to have been built from the same model as the famous sloop *Albert Baldwin.* She had been lengthened out in the process and whether this had any effect on her sailing qualities is questionable, but she was never as fast as people expected her to be. Gene Webster was the master for several years and the rivalry between him and Ben Paschal of the *Ervin J. Luce* was intense. The *Luce* was a slightly older vessel built at New London, Connecticut, in 1892, but somehow, she always seemed to take the *Bradford's* measure.

78. The *George R. Bradford* at Rockport, Massachusetts. Henry D. Fisher photo, Mystic Seaport Museum.

79. The *Ervin J. Luce* in her youth on Narragansett Bay. Edward W. Smith photo, Mystic Seaport Museum.

As freights became more scarce the two schooners were laid up at Rockport in the late twenties. The *Bradford* was finally sold to a firm of marine junk dealers in Portland and, for a time, Captain Les Bourget took her over, carrying any kind of cargoes that were offered. Later still, she was sold to go under Canadian registry and was engaged in the Sydney Mines–Newfoundland coal trade when the last war broke out.

The *Luce,* after a long lay-up, was reported sold back to her native Connecticut. She never reached there, however, for heavily loaded with sand, she sprang a leak when bound across Massachusetts Bay and capsized and sank. It was reported that she took at least one man down with her.

Celebrated among the down easters was the handsome *Mary E. Lynch,* a 185-ton schooner built at Newcastle, Maine, in 1890 for the West Indian fruit trade. She had the name of being very fast although somewhat ticklish to load. It was said she was a nightmare to steer if loaded ever so little by the head and, according to reports, her last skipper, unhappy at having her sold out from under him, so loaded her before the new owners came to take over. Witnesses declared that when she sailed, she was cutting figure eights all over the bay. In December of 1919 she was involved in a tragic accident. Loaded with granite, she was anchored near a stakeboat off the Jersey shore, opposite 32nd street on Manhattan. About 6:00 A.M. a tug ran into her and stove in her planking so she sank immediately, drowning four men out of a five-man crew in their bunks in the after cabin. She was later raised and repaired but was never rerigged and she became a gasoline scow at Boston.

The *Mabel E. Goss* was built originally in Nova Scotia at Port Greville under the name of *Lizzie B.* but was wrecked near Deer Isle and so completely rebuilt that she was granted a new documentation for the American coastwise trade. In her last years her skipper was Captain Mike Frazier, a rotund and jolly Frenchman. In the early twenties she was lost coming down over Sullivan "Falls" with a load of grout. She took a sheer in the strong current and piled up on the ledges, going to pieces before she could be salvaged.

The last schooner to be built particularly for the stone trade was the *Anna Sophia,* 146 net tons, launched at Dennysville by Lyman Pushee in 1923. In fact, she was one of the last two or three commercial schooners to be built in Maine. She was reported to have been built from a model whittled out by Ben Paschal, who left the *Ervin J. Luce* to become her first skipper. If true, it would appear he was a better skipper than ship designer, for he left her after only a trip or two and went back to the *Luce.* Captain George Eldridge of Machias took over the *Anna Sophia* but he was no happier with her than Paschal had been. She had a different hull than most coasters, having been built with a lot of drag to the keel which caused her to draw much more water aft than forward. Although only a little over 100 feet long, she had a beam of 30 feet and a stern as wide as that on many three-masters. She was slow and clumsy and a brute to steer, according to reports. She managed to survive a series of mishaps, however, and in the late twenties was owned in New York where, some time later, she had a pair of Diesel engines installed in her stern and went south to the West Indies.

Although built for general freighting, the old *Bloomer* became well-known as a stone drogher in her later years. Captain Ed Harper rigged a derrick boom and falls for her and in no time at all had all the business he could handle, building piers and freighting granite on short hauls to Rockland where it could be transshipped by rail or truck.

Despite her years, the *Bloomer* was in excellent condition for a coaster and Cap'n Ed was a smart and enterprising master. The vessel was built as a sloop in 1855 at Indian Point, Mt. Desert, and was constructed almost entirely of hackmatack, or "juniper," as it was called locally. She was framed and planked with it, and when she went to pieces after being abandoned nearly a hundred years later, she still had most of the plank and timber with which she was launched.

Cap'n Harper acquired her sometime in the nineties after selling the *Ella Eudora* in order to get a vessel with more carrying capacity. Originally the *Bloomer* was a typical down-east coaster with a short high poop that was some higher than the main deck bulwarks. A solid quarter rail enclosed it, and there were large wooden boat davits projecting over the stern. In later years this gave way to an open fly rail and iron davits, and at one time she had a flush afterhouse.

I believe Harper had a charter in 1898 to carry building material to forts being repaired or built in Boston Harbor. In order to increase the *Bloomer's* carrying capacity and to provide a dry place for the barrels of lime he carried in addition to sand, stone, brick and lumber, he extended the poop to form a sort of 'tween decks above the after part of the main deck. She had been built

80. The old *Bloomer* at rest in Rockland. Author's collection.

with a cutwater and billet head but this disappeared somewhere along the way, and I never knew her to have anything but an unadorned stem. Until about 1920 she had a bowsprit and flying jibboom, but after the jibboom carried away in a heavy breeze of wind, Cap'n Ed replaced it with a spike bowsprit that he made himself. In fact he made all the repairs and changes to the schooner and, while some of the work was pretty rough, it was strong, neat, and withstood the test of time. He needed few tools and relied mainly on broadaxe and adze. When he made the new bowsprit, he got the log, squared it, cut and tapered it to eight sides, then faired it off round and shouldered it for the various bands using only the simplest tools. A few passes with a plane finished the job.

From aloft, the *Bloomer* showed a deckline that was a perfect "cod's head and mackerel's tail." Her bows were bluff but rounded away under water, and she had a long, surprisingly fine run aft. With her outsize rig, it was small wonder that she could outsail many other vessels of her size. Cap'n Ed never missed a chance to sail by another schooner, and, even with no other vessel in sight, he never let the old girl loaf along easily. With full sail on, the *Bloomer* tore up the bay for hundreds of yards around and rolled white water up under her bow until it looked as though she were burrowing her way through a hillock of cotton wool.

More than twenty years later, when I ran across Freeman Closson while cruising with some friends down east, the talk turned to skippers and vessels we had known. In speaking of vessels with a reputation for some speed I said, "Well, Freeman, the old *Bloomer* could sail." His reply was, "Yup, she could sail all right, but, oh God, how she hated to!"

Her rig would make a modern designer shudder, and he would be sure to say she couldn't carry so much sail — but she did. She had two tall topmasts, limber as coachwhips, and never a backstay to her name. With both topsails set together with a fisherman staysail and jib topsail, those topmasts would almost tie themselves in knots but they never carried away. By all the rules of spar and rigging design she should have been dismasted every time it breezed on, but she carried the rig from about 1920 until she was dismantled more than a quarter century later. After Captain Harper's death, his son Austin — who had always gone with him — kept the schooner tied up at Spear's wharf at Rockland's north end, near his home. Visiting her every day, he kept her pumped out and aired and looked after her as though he were going to take her out the next week. He never did, however, and at last she was stripped of spars and gear, hauled onto the beach at Munroe Island, and left to the mercy of the elements. Even so, it took several years for her stout old hull to break up completely.

The *James A. Webster* was built particularly for the stone trade in 1890 at South Brooksville and was the last coaster to be built there. She was built for and sailed by Captain Albert Webster, hailing from Vinalhaven. Like the *Bloomer,* she worked only around the bay but, outside of a wood cargo or two in later years, she always plied in the stone trade. Just before the outbreak of World War II, Captain Webster put her into the dude cruise business and then sold her to go down to Long Island Sound, where she died some time later.

Among the larger schooners engaged almost exclusively in freighting stone were several vessels that actually hailed from

81. The *Charles Klinck,* one of several fine New London schooners to sail in the Maine stone trade. Courtesy Murray G. Peterson.

82. The *Annie B. Mitchell* flying light and almost becalmed. Courtesy
Roger C. Peterson.

New London, Connecticut, although they were always considered a part of the down-east fleet. These were the *George Klinck,* the *Charles Klinck,* the *William Booth* and the *Annie B. Mitchell.* Carlos Barry, of New London, was managing owner of them for several years, although the Booths of New London had a substantial interest in them and they were employed in hauling granite from the Booth-owned quarries down east to New York. They usually returned with coal for various Maine ports. The vessels were always kept in excellent condition and, without exception, were handsome examples of the rig.

When the stone trade came to an end, there was very little other business to be had, and the two *Klincks* and the *Annie B. Mitchell* were laid up in Rockland at Snow's shipyard. The *William Booth* had been lost following a collision with the four-master *Helen Barnet Gring* in 1928. The other vessels had undergone several changes of ownership, although nothing had been done to them and they had deteriorated substantially during the idle years.

The *George Klinck* was rescued from her mud berth about 1940 and was taken to Southwest Harbor by her new owners, Ledyard W. Sargent and others. There she was extensively rebuilt. On her first trip in 1941, however, she was literally torn apart in a gale off the Virginia capes, her crew being rescued in a dramatic operation by the U.S. aircraft carrier *Wasp.*

The *Charles Klinck* was sold to Nova Scotia but she fared little better, foundering in 1943. The *Annie B. Mitchell* remained tied up until after the war when she was stripped, towed to Andrews' Island off the Muscle Ridge Channel, and securely beached to become a lobster storage pound.

83. The *William Bisbee* in Penobscot Bay. Author's collection.

84. The stone sloop *America* with a load of granite in Boston Harbor. Courtesy Peabody Museum, Salem, Massachusetts.

Other three-masters in the stone trade were the *William Bisbee,* built at Rockland by I. L. Snow in 1902, and the *Lucy Evelyn,* which although built primarily for the lumber trade, carried a lot of granite in the later years.

The *Bisbee* was sold South and became a show ship, disguised as a pirate craft under the name of *José Gaspar.* As such, she was the headquarters for the Mystik Krew of Gasparilla, an organization devoted to the production of a Mardi Gras in the Florida city each year. She finally went to pieces in the fifties after she had deteriorated beyond the point of safety.

Of the stone sloops, none had been active to any extent after World War I. Several of them survived in one form or another and it was well into the late thirties before the *Albert Baldwin* was broken up in Smith's Cove in Gloucester as a W.P.A. project. The *America* became a water boat at T wharf in Boston, and the *Mary A. White* hung on to become a barge of some kind.

Down east, the *C. H. Edwards,* with a big two-story house built over her deck, became a floating machine shop for Howard and Horn of Portland for a number of years, and the *Yankee Girl* survived as a pulpwood barge. The *Alletta L. Hamilton,* better known as the *Letty,* was dropped from the register about the time of the First World War, while her "big sister," the *M. M. Hamilton,* continued in operation as a schooner, being bought, after the death of Captain Lynam, by a Professor Clapp at Duxbury, Massachusetts, where she became a floating zoological laboratory. She was finally hauled into shallow water at Clark's Island in Duxbury Bay and abandoned.

17 | SCOWS, JOHNNY-WOOD BO'TS, AND NOVIES

ALL along the coast were many odd types of craft engaged in some phase of the coasting trade. Most of them operated in local waters, having been designed for specific use in particular areas, like the Piscataqua River gundalows and the sailing scows that were once familiar sights around the Kennebec and Sheepscot Rivers. Other unusual types of craft that were familiar in Maine waters until comparatively late years were the New Brunswick wood schooners, called by everyone "Johnny wood bo'ts," since most of them came from the St. John River bringing a steady supply of kiln wood to towns around the bay where lime kilns were in operation.

The gundalows that plied the river separating Maine from New Hampshire actually ceased to operate shortly after the turn of the century, although one or two survivors lasted until about the time of the First World War. They were sailing scows of a peculiar type, very shoal draft with leeboards and a huge lateen sail, the only rig of this type surviving on the east coast of the United States into the twentieth century.

The Maine wood scows continued active much longer than the gundalows, and once were built by the scores, principally at various points along the Kennebec and upper Sheepscot Rivers. I believe the last working survivor was owned by a Captain Jones in the town of Sheepscot, above Wiscasset. For years, she made a couple of trips down river to Squirrel Island outside Boothbay Harbor with cordwood. She was requisitioned for government use at the outbreak of the Second World War.

There were several others in operation in the twenties and thirties, although there was very little business for them. One became a houseboat and when finally discarded, was hauled up astern of the old *Mary Weaver* at Boothbay and there she rotted away. Her name was the *Yankee Star* and she was last owned in her working career by Joe Jones of Newcastle, Maine.

These scows came into being chiefly because of the demand for cordwood and kiln wood along the coast and for bringing farm produce down the rivers to larger towns where it could be sold more readily. They could be built easily and cheaply and, since they had tremendous carrying capacity for their size, they were a paying investment for many years. They were simply square-

85. These sailing wood scows carried enormous loads of wood and up to the time of the first World War were a commonplace sight around the Kennebec, Sheepscot, and Damariscotta rivers and in the Penobscot Bay area.

ended, flat-bottomed sailing scows ranging in size from 45 feet to as much as 60 feet in length, although 50 feet was nearer the average. The beam was about one third of the length and the depth of hold seldom more than 3 or 4 feet. The sides were straight and the ends slanted up fore and aft in a strong rake from bottom to deckline. Most of them had a fair amount of sheer, and aft a skeg was built on to which the big rudder was attached. The steering arrangement was the same sort of block and tackle arrangement found in the older schooners, with the running part of the tackle wound around the wooden drum on the wheel shaft, although the purchase of the tackle led outboard to the trailing edge of the rudder.

There were no bulwarks although most had a low log rail running around the deck, and there was always provision for setting up the tall stakes along the sides to confine the tremendous deckloads of wood. There was an afterhouse large enough to give shelter to two men, similar to the accommodations found in a small bay coaster.

They were, as far as I ever knew, invariably sloop-rigged with a big single jib and mainsail, and some of the larger ones even set a gaff topsail. The bowsprit was a large square timber projecting over the bow for several feet, and it sometimes doubled as a cathead for the anchor. Its heel was let into a samson post that projected upward 2 or 3 feet through the deck and was used as a mooring bitt. Some sort of windlass was used on the larger scows, although few of them used chain anchor rodes. They usually tied up to a wharf or were grounded on the bank and seldom took more than a day to make their trips, so the ground tackle was not elaborate.

They carried a high deckload, and it was customary for the second man to stay on top of it and give directions to the man at the wheel who, more often than not, was steering completely blind, since the deckload was high as his head and came out to the sides of the craft.

Most of them operated up and down the rivers from the Kennebec to the Georges, but at least one in the later years hailed from Rockland and was steadily employed as a "kiln-wooder." She was the *Florence A. Harndon,* a 50-foot scow built in Woolwich, Maine, in 1892.

In 1911 the big 70-foot *Umbajejus,* one of the largest scows built on the Kennebec, took several loads of piling to Boston. She was nine weeks making the first trip and nearly as long on the succeeding ones.

In the early days there were many other unusual types; quite recently concrete evidence of one of these ancient craft was located at South Bristol. Murray G. Peterson, a naval architect living at Jones' Cove, became curious about some old waterlogged timbers sunk in the shoal water on his property at the head of the cove. One or two of the older residents of the town thought a pinky had been hauled in there and left to die but close examination proved it to be a type of craft even older. The timbers were hauled out on dry land and gave strong evidence that the little vessel, about 40 feet long, had perhaps been a Chebacco (Essex, Massachusetts) "dogbody." This was a colonial type of craft, a direct descendant

86. A "Johnny-wood bo't" of the older type.

on the still earlier shallop. They were cat-rigged schooners almost like an overgrown ship's boat but decked, or partially decked, over and had a deeper hull. They seem to have originated in the vicinity of Chebacco Parish, later Essex, in the early 1700s and were used for fishing and coasting.

The timbers found by Mr. Peterson left no doubt that the craft was very old and had originally been built of hand-hewed timbers and fastened with wood treenails (trunnels) throughout. The stem was a huge knee, hewed out of a piece of solid oak and having a mast step cut into it, indicating that the foremast must have been set only inches aft of the stem. There was no sign of any place for a bobstay fastening such as would have appeared had the craft been rigged with a bowsprit, and the few iron bolts or spikes in the hull indicated they had obviously been added in later years. The frames were built up in single, overlapping futtocks, such as was the fashion in colonial days, and a pile of fire-scarred bricks indicated she had once had a fireplace for cooking. Also, it was known the original owner of the property, for whom the cove was named, came there from Essex about 1800 and it is not unreasonable to believe the old wreck may be a colonial craft of nearly 200 years of age.

Similar in type, although much larger, were the St. John (New Brunswick) wood boats. Of all the unusual craft that sailed Maine coastal waters, these "Johnny-wood bo'ts" are among the best remembered. Although Canadian built and owned, they made their living for many years bringing tremendous loads of kiln wood from New Brunswick to Thomaston, Rockland and Rockport. At one time they were as well known as any of the local vessels and, at the height of the trade, there were scores of them. Mostly, they were built on the St. John River and were just about the minimum in vessel construction. They were "colorful" craft, for the woods used in their construction were black spruce, yellow birch, and red oak. Such woods are very susceptible to rot from fresh-water dampness, and in about seven years they usually had to be extensively rebuilt. Labor was cheap, however, and some of them kept going for more years than one would believe possible.

Originally, they were rigged as cat schooners, the foremast being stepped right up "in the eyes" of the hull and the rudder hung "outdoors" on the broad, flat transom. They, like the Essex dogbodies, looked like an overgrown ship's boat or shallop and, as a matter of fact, it is not unlikely that all these local types stemmed from a common ancestor. Other outstanding features of the "Johnny-wood bo'ts" were the big, square afterhouses, whose floors were on the main deck; the movable galley, or cookhouse, lashed down to ringbolts on deck, so it could be moved at will; and the crude wooden boat davits projecting out over the stern.

Strangely enough, these odd vessels were extremely good sailers off the wind for they had a long, sloping run in the afterbody and, with the big foresail and mainsail "wung out" to balance each other, they could slide "down hill" at an amazing rate of speed. Some of them, when rebuilt in the later years, were given a more conventional rig, and a few were built and rigged with the foremast set back in normal position and a bowsprit and flying jibboom added.

Two of the last survivors of this type were the *D. W. B.*, built at Westfield, New Brunswick, and the *Eskimo,* also built on the

St. John River but hailing from Parrsboro, Nova Scotia, in later years. The *Eskimo* was working in the later twenties and was known all along the Maine coast and in the Boston area where she brought many loads of cordwood or piling. She even ventured down over the shoals to New York or Long Island Sound ports. She was rigged as a conventional one-topmast coaster with bowsprit and flying jibboom. Her stern, however, was like the earlier vessels of the type, the huge rudder being hung "outdoors" on heavy, hand-forged pintles and gudgeons and the tiller extending inward through the open taffrail. It was controlled by the usual block and tackle arrangement. Her original wooden boat davits had been replaced by iron ones, but she had the high afterhouse, and the galley was located in the movable deckhouse, usually lashed on deck between the fore and mainmasts.

In deep water parlance, Nova Scotia and New Brunswick vessels were usually spoken of as "Bluenoses," but along the coast they were more frequently called "Novies." Many of the regular schooners from the lumber ports of the Minas Basin and elsewhere were almost as well known to Maine coastermen as they were in their home waters. They were handsome little schooners, some of them being half way between coasters and fishermen in design, embodying the best-looking features of both types. This type was usually designated as "tern" schooners in the Provinces, although technically "tern" formerly meant any three-masted schooner.

Nearly all the Nova Scotia schooners were good-looking, and, although built of soft wood and sometimes short-lived, many of them were remarkably fast. One, the *Rose Anne Belliveau,* a little three-master hailing from Belliveau Cove near Weymouth,

87. The *Eskimo* loaded with piling about 1920. Courtesy John Quincy Adams.

88. The ill-fated *Ena F. Parsons*. Courtesy Peabody Museum, Salem, Massachusetts.

Nova Scotia, set a record for sailing which I doubt has ever been equaled before or since by a vessel of anywhere near her size and type. With a full cargo of lumber aboard, she sailed from her home port for Boston about 1923 and made the 300-mile passage in exactly twenty-four hours. This figures out to an average of better than 12 knots, and while that speed would not be unusual for a blue water ship running her easting down or a big fisherman running home from the banks, it is astounding for a little coaster of less than 125 feet in length.

Well-known in Maine waters were the three-masted schooners owned by George Parsons of Parrsboro, particularly the *Ena* and *Frances Parsons*. Both of these vessels loaded about a quarter million feet of square-edged lumber for trips to Boston and New York and operated for years with steamerlike regularity. The *Ena F. Parsons* was lost in October, 1933 under tragic circumstances when she capsized and drowned all hands. Capt. Daniel Desmond was master at the time. The *Frances Parsons* was lost off Bermuda about 1943.

The *Frederick P. Elkins,* built in 1919 in the Minas Basin as the *Seaman A. O.,* was a regular visitor to Maine and Massachusetts waters, as was the *Stewart T. Salter.* The latter ran steadily in the lumber trade to Boston until at last she was laid up in Chelsea Creek at East Boston with the tide coming and going in her hull at will. Some optimistic soul from down east, however, went to work on her and she lived to go South in the thirties, rigged as a "bald-headed" auxiliary under the name of *Caroline.*

The *Marine,* of 511 tons, was larger than many of the Nova

Scotiamen, built in response to the demand for wartime tonnage in 1919, and after the war was over she continued to operate in the coastwise lumber trade until well into the thirties.

By contrast the little *Mary B. Brooks* was only 246 tons but for many years she ran steadily in the lumber trade during the summer and went to the West Indies in the winter. She was wrecked down there and made a last appearance in a moving picture in the late thirties.

The *Peaceland* was another well-known regular in the lumber trade from the Minas Basin. She was built at Annapolis Royal and hailed from that town, lasting until the Second World War. Two other very well-known Nova Scotiamen were the *Minas King* and the *Minas Prince.* Both were built in the closing years of the First World War, the *King* being launched at Bass River. She was skippered by Captain George Merriam for most of her career. The *Prince* was built at Spencer's Island and lasted until 1940, when she was lost while bound to New Haven, Connecticut, with a load of plaster rock. She was then under command of Captain Murray Willigar, but for most of her career, Wallace Smith had been the master. She was a money maker for her owners, being a good carrier and smart enough to make excellent passages. Of 506 gross tons, register, she could take something over 900 tons of plaster rock. Her lumber capacity was about half a million feet on the average, somewhat more if the cargo was spruce or other light lumber and less if it was heavy stuff. One hundred and fifty-two cords of pulpwood was about maximum for that type of cargo. Once, on a trip to Boston, while being towed to her discharge wharf, she got jammed in the railroad bridge at Neponset, bringing all passenger train traffic to a halt for the rest of the day.

One of the smallest of these Nova Scotia three-masters was the *Ronald C. Longmire,* built at Meteghan in 1921. She was owned by W. R. Longmire of Annapolis Royal and ran quite steadily with building lumber to Gloucester and Salem, Massachusetts. In 1933 she was driven ashore at Salem during a gale, and for a time it looked as though she had come to the end of her career, but she was got off and continued in the lumber trade for several more years.

Two other handsome three-masters from the Bay of Fundy were the *Whiteway* and *Westway.* Both were built in the Minas Basin in later years and both used to carry lumber more or less regularly during the summer months to the Hutchinson Lumber Co. at Lynn, Massachusetts. In the winter they frequently loaded salt fish for Barbados and returned home with salt from Turks Island or one of the other salt cays. It is interesting to one who remembers these vessels to see that a new express highway that cuts across the Lynn waterfront now covers the wharves where these vessels used to lie. One of the last schooners ever to bring a cargo of lumber to the Hutchinson Lumber Co. wharf was the old *City of New York,* first a Norwegian whaler, bark-rigged, later an exploration vessel in the Byrd Antarctic expedition, and lastly, a three-masted schooner in the lumber trade owned and commanded by Captain Lou Kenedy, widely known all around the western Atlantic as a colorful character whose adventures might have qualified him to figure in books such as those written by Jack London or Ernest Hemingway.

There were also a few two-masters that were as much at home in American waters and ports as they were in the Bay of Fundy. The *Margery Austin* was a handsome little 128-tonner, built at Harvey Bank, New Brunswick, in 1918 for a Captain Robinson. She was wrecked on her first trip out when only a few miles from her home port, and for a time it looked as though her career would be over before it started, but they got her off the rocks and rebuilt her and thereafter she carried on a long and successful career.

The *Vilda A.* was another two-sticker of about the same type and size as the *Austin,* although she was not so handsome a vessel. On one of her later trips in the twenties she lost her deckload in a gale of wind in the Gulf of Maine and was finally picked up and towed into Portland, floating on her hold full of lumber. She was repaired and went to sea again but did not last many more years. One of the last surviving smaller schooners was the *Rayo,* built about 1920, which used to bring 75,000 to 80,000 feet of spruce to Quincy, Massachusetts, quite often during the decade following the first war. Young Elijah Neves was master and, reversing the usual procedure, his father went with him in the capacity of cook. The *Rayo* was still in service in 1940, although a pair of gasoline engines had been installed in her stern and her rig was reduced. One engine had substantially more power than the other, so under power she had a marked tendency at times to go off crabwise.

Some of these engine installations were pretty crude jobs and were seldom very successful. Oddly enough, they didn't seem to be an efficient "improvement," and towing with a power yawl-boat was preferred by most skippers.

I recall one race when I was in the *George W. Collins.* We had sheltered overnight in Bass Harbor in company with a much bigger Nova Scotiaman, the *Wm. H. Waters.* Next morning it was light weather and we put our yawl-boat down, and, after getting sail set, started the "one lunger." The engine had originally been a 5 h.p. Eagle but it had parts from several other makes on it and it coughed, sputtered and banged as though it were going to give up the ghost any minute. In any event, we started out with it and, at the same time, the *Waters* got under way. She had two similar but larger engines in her stern and to hear them one would have supposed them to be 50 h.p. apiece. However, we pulled away from her steadily and, although we were depending almost entirely on the yawl-boat for propulsion, the *Waters* never did catch up.

18 | UP TO THE WEST'ARD

THE Maine coasting fleet in the later years was divided into three categories — "Bay coasters," "Boston coasters" and the others which ventured around Cape Cod to ports further along the coast. Most of this latter group went no further than New York, although some of the larger vessels still went to the Gulf Coast and, occasionally, to the West Indies.

Bay coasters were usually the smaller vessels of 30 to 70 tons, operating in the pulpwood or cordwood trade around Penobscot Bay and running as packets to and from Portland. Few of them went beyond the limits of the St. Croix River to the east and Cape Elizabeth to the west.

Boston coasters were generally the two-masters, 75 to 150 tons, although there were some small three-masters whose owners preferred to work east of Cape Cod. In an earlier day many vessels of this type and size had worked the whole length of the coast into the Gulf of Mexico and down to the West Indies. By the time of the First World War, however, most of the vessels were old, as were their owner-skippers, and there were few cargoes for them to bring from the south.

Most of the New York fleet were three-masters, although in the area around Machias and Calais — from whence a great deal of building lumber was shipped to New York — there were many big two-masted schooners of close to, or over, 200 tons. Some skippers seemed to feel they were more easily loaded and handled than a three-master in the lumber trade. There were also a number of big two-masters freighting granite and plaster rock to New York.

Cape Cod was the western limit of the Boston coaster's operation, but for the New York-bound vessels it marked the beginning of the hardest part of the westward passage. Even in good weather the passage "down over the shoals" is to be made with some degree of caution. The long crooked miles of channels wind their way between shoals that have been death traps for vessels and men since the earliest days of the coasting trade. The beginning of the east-west passage was at Pollock Rip lightship where the tidal currents run strongly through Pollock Rip Slue. From there, the channel wanders down by Pollock Rip Shoal, Stone Horse, the Handkerchief, Hedge Fence, Cross Rip, and the rest, all of them deadly to a vessel unfortunate enough to fetch up on one of them in bad weather.

Eastbound sailing vessels would attempt the passage only if wind and tide were right, for no one wanted to anchor on the shoals if it could be avoided. Sometimes, however, a shift of wind or a sudden fog might force a vessel to anchor, which to many skippers was still preferable to working a long way back to the shelter of Vineyard Haven.

The danger of being run down by a steamer had abated when the Cape Cod canal was put through but there was always danger of collision with another sailing vessel or, if a gale blew up, of dragging anchor or parting the chain. All the shoals were well marked by lightships or buoys, and lifesaving stations were spaced at short intervals all along the Cape Cod outer shore.

The tale of vessels and men lost is a long one, nevertheless. In 1928 the three-master *William Booth,* westbound with a load of stone, went to the bottom following a collision with the big four-master *Helen Barnet Gring.* Four years before, in March, the giant six-master *Wyoming* went to her doom, taking Captain Charles Glaesel and his crew of fourteen down with her. She was eastbound with a load of coal and was forced to anchor near the Handkerchief. During the night, she apparently dragged down on the shoal, struck and burst open, although some had the theory that her anchor chains sawed down through the hull to the waterline. In any event, no one lived to tell the story, and it was some time even before they found identifiable wreckage to confirm her loss.

In 1921, the *Henry F. Kreger,* a four-master loaded with gypsum for New York, stranded on Pollock Rip Shoal. The crew panicked and took to the boat, leaving the captain and mate aboard.

The crew were picked up by the schooner *Augusta G. Hilton* and were subsequently taken ashore by a lifeboat from the Great Point station on Nantucket. The captain and mate were rescued from the doomed *Kreger* by a Coast Guard cutter just before the vessel broke up.

Not long before, the schooner *Isaiah K. Stetson* of Bangor was caught by rapidly worsening weather while attempting the eastbound passage of the shoals. She was deep-loaded with coal and anchored to windward of the Handkerchief. As the gale increased, her anchor chain parted and in minutes she was hard and fast aground, the seas making a clean breach over her. Four of her crew were swept to their deaths before the Coast Guard cutter *Acushnet* appeared and sent a boat to pick up Captain William Richard and Seaman Joe Watkins, the only survivors.

Albert and Freeman Closson, brothers and both coasting captains, had a narrow escape in the last days of coasting under sail. They were homeward bound from New York in the big two-topmaster *Storm Petrel,* much too large a vessel for two men to handle despite their combined years of experience. Business had been poor and the brothers had taken her out on shares, gambling to make a few dollars by eliminating the expense of crew's wages. It was the sort of operation not too difficult in summer when undertaken by two experienced men, but in the winter it was a gamble all the way.

They had run by Vineyard Haven, hoping to get over the shoals without lying over, but they were finally forced to anchor to await the turn of the tide. In the meantime, the wind shifted and before long it was a blizzard. With sails furled and gear icing up

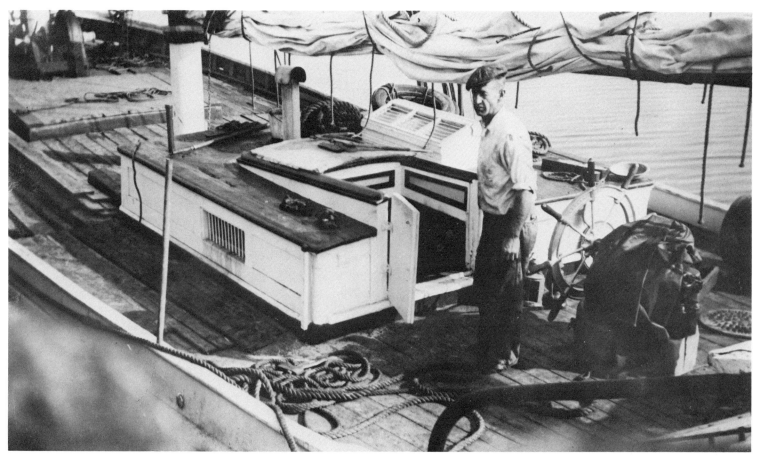

89. Captain Claude Tucker on the quarterdeck of his little *Coral*.
Courtesy Charles F. Sayle.

90. The oddly-named *Tansy Bitters* with a deck load on Long Island Sound. Author's collection.

91. The ancient sloop *Wasp* at John Beattie's Leete Island quarry in 1893. Courtesy Robert Beattie.

fast, there was nothing for them to do but hang onto their anchors and pray the chains didn't part. Fortunately someone noted their plight and got word to the Coast Guard. A cutter reached them, helped them get their anchors, and towed them to shelter in Vineyard Haven. They finally got the vessel home to Ellsworth, but the experience convinced them that sailing too shorthanded in an overloaded old vessel was hardly worth the effort. In relating the story Freeman Closson said he was absolutely convinced at one point they would never make it.

In the heyday of sail, there was usually a powerful tug standing by in Vineyard Haven to aid vessels in trouble, and the crews of the lifesaving stations strung along the outer Cape shore were always available to render assistance. In those days they never restricted their efforts to saving life. They would board a grounded vessel, aid in running out anchors, securing gear, and if it was possible to haul a schooner off "by her own bootstraps," they worked like heroes to that end. The surfmen and keepers of the old U.S. Life-Saving Service were men who truly deserved the title of heroes. In the long history of that "graveyard of ships" — the shoals that border the "elbow" and "upper arm" of Cape Cod — the men of the Life-Saving Service, and later the U.S. Coast Guard, proved their worth time and again. The scores of names of men lost in the performance of their duty bears witness to the dedication of those whose every effort was directed toward the rescue of others in peril aboard countless vessels all along the coast. The stations along the shores of Long Island had more than their share of work as did the surfmen who manned the stations every few miles along the terrible Jersey beaches.

Once into Vineyard Sound, the down-east coaster began to meet some of her opposite numbers, even in the later years when the ranks of the Long Island Sound coasting fleet had been decimated. Almost never in the twenties did any of the smaller sound vessels appear to the eastward of Cape Cod. A number of three-masters like the *William Booth, Annie B. Mitchell,* and the two *Klincks,* as well as the *Charles C. Lister* and *Abbie C. Stubbs,* voyaged regularly to Maine to bring back stone from the various quarries owned by the Booth interests in New London or building lumber from the most easterly ports.

Working steadily in the New Bedford, Nantucket, and Vineyard Haven area was the handsome little *Coral,* owned and skippered by Captain Claude Tucker. She registered only 32 tons and had been built in 1878 at Port Jefferson, Long Island, by J. M. Bayles. In her later years, she had an auxiliary engine in her stern but Captain Tucker always sailed if there was wind enough to give her steerage way. She was eventually a victim of the 1938 hurricane, being so badly damaged that she was not worth repairing. Hauled up beside an old wharf in Fairhaven, she finally went to pieces, although traces of her "bones" may be seen there today.

Until he bought the *Alice S. Wentworth* in 1921, Zeb Tilton could usually be spotted around the islands or the upper end of the sound in the *John B. Norris,* a 46-tonner which he sold to Calais, Maine, just before buying the *Wentworth.*

An oddly named little schooner working upper Long Island Sound was the *Tansy Bitters.* Her owner-skipper Sam Collins had installed a gas engine in her also, although he, too, preferred to sail whenever possible. Another schooner with auxiliary power

92. Captain Zeb Tilton, most famous of all coasting skippers in the Vineyard Sound–Buzzards area. Courtesy Charles F. Sayle.

was the diminutive *Herman L. Rogers* of only 25 tons, built in 1889 at Stonybrook, New York. During her last years, she was owned and operated in the Buzzard's Bay region. Captain Ben Waterworth had her for several years, but at last sold her to a tyro who soon hauled her up in Parkwood Creek at Wareham where she went to pieces.

Remembered by all coastermen who frequented the Long Island Sound area was the *Altana M. Jagger*, a 126-ton two-master built in 1890 at Wilmington, Delaware for Captain Charles Emmett and others of Westerly and Providence, Rhode Island. In her later years Captain Fred C. Smith had her and operated her successfully. She was presumably named for the wife of one of the original owners and the name was unusual enough to stick in the minds of those who had seen it on the stern.

The custom of naming vessels for some person connected with the ownership was a common one. Most of the names were commonplace as are the names of people in any average community. Occasionally, however, some unusual name served to endow a vessel with a special sort of distinction. The *Jagger* was one of these, but once when I mentioned the subject to a skipper during a passage down the sound, he told me of a vessel with a name that still intrigues me when I think of it — the *Alfaretta S. Snare*, built in 1881 at Bath, Maine, for Captain W. E. Snare and others. Outside the realm of personal names, I think the prize for the most unusual name must be awarded to a 12-ton schooner built in 1881 at Lockport, New York, across whose stern was lettered the name *Merchant's Gargling Oil*!

To get back to the *Jagger,* she had distinctions other than

93. The *Altana M. Jagger* bound up Narragansett Bay in her early
days. Edward W. Smith photo, Mystic Seaport Museum.

her unusual name. She was unusually narrow of beam and had the name of being "tender" in a breeze, particularly when light. Making a run down the sound in the big *Lavolta,* deep-loaded with stone, we fell in company with the *Jagger* just about the time a squall struck. We hardly rolled a full strake down, but she went over until we almost expected to see her keel come out of water. Fred Smith was in her at the time, but he has since told me that he never worried about her going over. He felt that if she was going to capsize, she would have done so long since. It bothered her original skipper, Captain Emmett, for he only kept her about a year and then left to take over the big *Harriet C. Whitehead,* built for him at Waterford, Connecticut. By contrast, she was so stiff that anyone below had to come on deck to find out what tack she was on, according to those who had sailed in her.

The *Jagger* was also unusual in having a shin-cracker, an antiquated steering wheel for a schooner built in 1890. Some of the old whalers and schooners stuck to them, but a fixed wheel either with blocks and tiller ropes or one of the patent geared wheels was much preferred.

The *Jagger* was extensively engaged in running moulding sand from the Hudson River to Providence and Taunton. She was owned principally in Providence in her later years, operating under the management of Allen Gurney. As was mentioned earlier, one of her last skippers, following Fred Smith as master, was Captain Arthur Stevens, former owner and master of the *Alice S. Wentworth* and the *Frank Brainerd.*

The *Harriet C. Whitehead* worked around the sound until the late twenties and was then sold to Chesapeake Bay to enter the Virginia lumber trade. She survived to be converted to a power vessel and was lost at sea in 1944.

Also working on the sound in later years were a couple of survivors of the once-numerous "brownstone fleet" which had carried the material for the Fifth Avenue mansions from the quarries on the Connecticut River to New York. These were the *Brownstone,* 167 tons, built as the *Fannie G. Warner* at Hartford, in 1869, and the *Helen P.,* 101 tons, built at East Haddam, Connecticut, in 1864. Several vessels from this trade had been sold down east in the years previously, among them the *Gilbert Stancliff* and the *Frank Brainerd.*

It was at about this time that the Leete Island quarry operation came to an end. John Beattie of Clinton, Connecticut, had started the business before the Civil War, and at one time owned a number of vessels, among them an ancient Hudson River sloop named *Wasp,* 69 tons, built at Lansingburg, New York, in 1813. In her last years she was a lighter, being towed, but earlier she had sailed from the quarries at Leete Island carrying stone for many of the wharves, walls, and other construction in the New York harbor area. The family carried on the business for several years after John Beattie's death, and the last two survivors of their fleet were the schooners *Tom Beattie,* built in 1886 at Bath, Maine, and the *American Eagle,* launched originally as the *Three Brothers* at Tuckahoe, New Jersey, in 1873. As was the case with many coasters, she was so completely rebuilt at Northport, Long Island, in 1899 that she was awarded a new documentation.

Two of the last sailing coasters on the sound were the schooners *J. Lloyd Hawkridge* and the *Robert Jno. Beswick.* Both vessels

94. The big *Harriet C. Whitehead* in the Pawcatuck River. Courtesy Mr. Robert Emmett.

95. The *J. Lloyd Hawkridge* — one of the last sailing coasters on Long Island
Sound. A Frank Karppi photo from the Peabody Museum collection.

had been built at Milford, Delaware, the former in 1905 and the latter in 1901. Both later hailed from New Haven, the *Hawkridge* owned by Captain Irving DeWick, and the latter by Daniel Walls. The *Beswick* in her last years was converted to a power lighter, but Captain DeWick kept the *Hawkridge* under sail until the beginning of the Second World War when he sold her and retired. She went South and was lost shortly afterwards. Prior to purchasing the *Hawkridge,* Captain DeWick had the handsome little Hudson River schooner *Henrietta Collyer,* 56 tons, built at Nyack, New York, in 1880. The *Ella,* 53 tons, built in 1869 at Northport, New York, was owned by members of the same family. They sold her down east in later years, and, after working around Penobscot Bay in the pulpwood trade for a number of years, she was hauled up on the beach at Carney Island, Little Deer Isle, and abandoned. Until recently, her hull was intact, although the tide flowed freely in and out of her gaping seams.

There were a few other small schooners working in the sound after the First World War, many of them with auxiliaries installed, but they were far outnumbered by the vessels hailing from Maine. The *Laforrest L. Simmons* of 104 tons was built in Milford, Delaware, in 1909 but had been owned in Fall River, Massachusetts, for many years. She was at last sold to the Chesapeake where she continued to sail for many more years. Reversing the usual procedure, the handsome little *Alida Hearn* came North from the Chesapeake to hail from Patchogue and engage in the Long Island Sound coasting trade. The *Grace P. Willard,* 101 tons, built in Mystic in 1891, was also among the survivors around the sound, although she came to her end shortly after the war. The *B. F. Jayne,* a 59-tonner built in 1883 hailed from Fall River in her later years and was in service until the later twenties. The *Caroline Butler* of 47 tons was built and owned in New London but was owned in the late twenties by O. A. Gilbert of Boston. The vessel beside which she is lying in the illustration was a most unusual craft. She was a three-masted semi-scow-type schooner named *Witch Hazel,* registering 239 tons, built in Bath, Maine, in 1872. At the time the photograph was taken, she was owned in New London. She was lost by stranding near New Haven in November, 1911, while bound from New York to Providence. The captain and two of his crew were drowned.

A familiar 71-ton two-master in the sound was the old *A. G. Pease,* built for the brownstone trade at Middletown, Connecticut, away back in 1854. She was bought by Portuguese owners for the Cape Verde packet trade but did not survive for any length of time. Old coasters very frequently wound up in the hands of Portuguese owners for this particular business. Profits from the trade between New Bedford and the Cape Verde Island were great if the vessels survived the crossing, but all too often they failed to do so. The Cape Verde Islanders — whether living there or in New Bedford — seldom had large capital to invest in good vessels, so they bought old coasters and fishermen to carry the passengers and freight to and from the islands.

About 1920 they dredged up the schooner *Oakwoods,* which had been sunk in Buzzard's Bay following a collision with a U.S. submarine, and rebuilt her at Fairhaven, Massachusetts, renaming

96. The little *Caroline Butler* alongside the unusual semi-scow-type
three-master *Witch Hazel* in the Mystic River. The *Dart* is upriver.
E.A. Scholfield photo, Mystic Seaport Museum.

her for that town. She had originally been built at Kennebunk in 1880 but she was granted the documentation of a new vessel in 1921. She did not last long in the packet trade, however.

Two old two-masted coasters were bought for the trade from down-east owners. They were the *Ernst T. Lee,* 139 tons, built at Calais, Maine, in 1873 and the *T. W. Allan,* 95 tons, built at Dennysville, Maine, in 1870. The *Lee* sailed from New Bedford in January, 1920, and shortly afterward had to be abandoned when her seams opened and she began to take in water faster than it could be pumped out. Fortunately her crew and passengers were picked up by a passing ship and returned to New Bedford. The *Allan* was not so lucky. She had sailed from New Bedford in November of 1919 with eighteen in the crew and eight passengers under the command of Captain James Silva. More than a month later, identifiable wreckage from her drifted ashore in Nova Scotia, indicating that she had been lost with all hands.

In those years following World War I, every vessel which went to New York was consigned to a favorite broker. Many of the New York brokers were originally from Maine, and, while the business for sailing coasters was diminishing inexorably, they still made every effort to find eastbound cargoes for them when they arrived. J. A. Elliot & Co. was started by one of the family in the Dunn & Elliot firm of Thomaston, Maine. W. E. Crockett & Co. had a down-east background as did several others. Gilmartin & Trundy (later Gilmartin & Co.), Homer & Puddington, Pendleton Bros., Scammell Bros., and J. F. Whitney were among the principal brokers with whom the down-east schooner owners and skippers dealt.

In Boston, Crowell & Thurlow, John G. Hall & Co., and John S. Emery & Co. handled most of the larger sailing vessels, while the Boston Ship Brokerage Co. (O. A. Gilbert) and David Simpson handled the smaller vessels. It must have been an exasperating enterprise in those last years. Freights were low and cargoes, particularly those to the eastward, were difficult to find. The broker was often expected to be a combination of Father Confessor, bail bondsman, and even welfare agent when a trip proved to be financially disastrous. They made money only because almost every down-east skipper seemed to realize that he had to ultimately rely on the brokers to keep his vessel in operation.

97. The *Abbie S. Walker*, old but still beautiful. Courtesy John Quincy Adams.

19 | SOME THREE-MASTERS

COASTERMEN, like seamen everywhere, appreciate good looks in a vessel, and while there was wide disagreement as to individual schooners, it was generally conceded that the three-masted rig was the handsomest of all. It has balance, both in looks and in handling, and in schooners from 200 to 300 tons, it was more easily handled than most two-masters of the same size, or even smaller.

Good looks in vessels was the subject of endless debate on wharves, in ship chandleries, and during ship-visiting sessions. It would be impossible to make a definite choice from among even the comparatively few survivors of the coasting fleet in the decade following World War I. Generally speaking, the older schooners were the better looking, being finer-lined, longer-sparred and more highly decorated. Very little artistic effort was wasted on schooners built after the turn of the century and their hulls and rigs were designed with an eye for carrying capacity and ease of handling.

In the later years, of course, many of the old-timers like the *John Bracewell* were losing their shape and suffering from general deterioration. For a time, some of them were kept in reasonably good shape and showed plenty of evidence that they were once gems of commercial naval architecture, but many others had lost whatever pretensions they once might have had to beauty.

Foremost among the better-looking schooners was the little *Abbie S. Walker,* launched at Jonesboro, Maine, in 1883. She was tall-sparred with long topmasts and a long flying jibboom, and her green-painted hull kept some of its original sheer right up to the end.

The year 1883 also marked the launch of another handsome little three-master, the *Mattie J. Alles* of 229 tons built at Yarmouth, Maine, for John Alles of Boston and others. She was named for his wife, and her first master was another member of the family, Captain George Crockett of Portland. A photograph of her on the stocks just before launching shows an extremely handsome little schooner with comparatively fine lines and a well-proportioned rig. A grandson and namesake of the original John Alles tells me, however, that it was a family tradition that the *Mattie* never made a dime for her owners. Captain Crockett was apparently no driver and spent a lot on the schooner. In later years, when she was owned in Machias under command of Captain L. B. Wallace, she seemed to do better financially and paid good dividends as long as there was any business to be had. When I first knew her, she was still a handsome little schooner, retaining much of her original sheer and always appearing neat and trim. Later on she was sold to Jonesport and at last to New York owners. By the later twenties, she had deteriorated markedly and was looking "pretty well run-out," as the down-east expression goes. She disappeared from the register shortly afterwards.

Also considered to be a good-looking three-master was the *Frank Brainerd,* built at Rockland, Maine, in 1908. She was a centerboarder, intended to carry brownstone from the Connecticut River to New York, and was very heavily constructed. When this trade came to an end, she entered the general coasting trade and joined the down-east fleet in carrying lumber, laths, and granite to the westward, going back east with coal. Captain Arthur Stevens bought her to replace the *Alice S. Wentworth,* after he sold her in 1921. He did well with her for a few years but she eventually got ashore in Frenchman's Bay, and the salvage bills ran so high that he finally had to relinquish her ownership to Merritt Ober of Rockland.

She continued to operate between Maine and New York as long as there was any business, but eventually she was sold to Portuguese owners to enter the Cape Verde packet trade. In the middle thirties she sailed from Providence for the islands but had to be abandoned when about halfway across, her crew and passengers being taken off by the U.S. Coast Guard.

I. L. Snow & Co. of Rockland not only built some fine vessels but owned and operated them successfully. One of the earlier three-masters and by all odds, the handsomest, was the 354-ton *Lavinia M. Snow,* built in 1893. She was beautifully proportioned and a fine example of the down-east shipbuilder's art. She was well cared for and despite several accidents, retained her original sheer and handsome appearance right to the end. In 1920, she got ashore at Abaco in the Bahamas but was later floated only to become involved a year later in a collision with the lighthouse tender *Azalea* near Pollock Rip Lightship. Captain Steve Peabody was her master until Snow sold her to Captain John Stevens of Rockland, former owner of the *Gilbert Stancliff.* There is a slight coincidence in the fact that both Captain John Stevens and Captain Arthur Stevens (no relationship) should sell two-masters and purchase three-masters, thereby suffering serious financial loss as a result. Captain John Stevens lost the *Lavinia* on Hatteras not long after buying her, and, since she was not covered by insurance, it was a hard blow.

It was clearly a case of hard luck for both skippers for each was competent and careful and kept his schooner in prime shape. Captain John Stevens had been master of several of Snow's vessels, including their brig the *Caroline Gray* in the West Indian trade. After spending several years in semiretirement, he took over one of Frank Swift's dude cruisers at Camden and continued in her until he was well over eighty, a heart attack finally forcing his retirement. He died shortly afterwards.

A later and somewhat larger three-master built by the Snow yard for their own account was the *Helvetia,* launched in 1905, registering 499 tons. She was not quite as handsome as some of

98. The *Mattie J. Alles*—too fine lined to carry a full cargo, she was
a good sailer but a poor money-maker. Courtesy Robert H.I. Goddard.

99. Schooner *Helvetia,* 499 tons. Built 1905 by I. L. Snow & Co. at Rockland, Maine, for their own account. Became a pulpwood barge in the 1930's. Author's collection.

the older schooners, but she was a good carrier and a good money maker for several years.

She continued in operation through the twenties but was then laid up at Rockland, and in 1933 was auctioned off at a marshal's sale for a paltry $755 to Capt. E. F. Pettigrew of Larrabee, Maine. In 1935 she set what must almost be a record for slow passages when she took twenty-one days from Nova Scotia to New York. During the Second World War she was taken over by the government with the intention of making her into a "Q" ship to decoy German submarines, but the war ended before she was ready. She finally went back to her home waters in Maine and, stripped of her spars and rigging, became a pulpwood barge, spending the rest of her days afloat being dragged up and down the coast at the end of a towline.

Snow also owned several other three-masters of their own construction during the later years of the coasting trade. Among them were the *Hugh De Payens,* lost off Cardenas, Cuba, in 1919; the *Metinic, Methebesec* and *Tarratine,* all of whom failed to survive the war.

The *Wawenock* lasted until 1929, when she was lost on Mc-Glathery's Island in Jericho Bay. She and two or three other Snow three-masters were notable for their high-raised forecastle decks which made them look like West Coasters forward. The crews liked this feature for it made them much dryer forward, but it certainly did nothing for their looks.

During the First World War, a number of large three-masters of better than 500 tons were built at various places along the Maine coast, and some of them survived until the last years of the trade. Very few of them had any pretensions to good looks, however, and most of them were so large they were not profitable to operate on the short hauls between Maine and Boston, or even New York. In the last years, some of them entered the Nova Scotia lumber trade and did fairly well, although by that time they were usually under Nova Scotian registry.

Some of these larger three-masters built just before or during World War I survived until the Second World War, among them the *Edward R. Smith,* lost in January, 1943; the *Albert H. Willis,* almost a sister ship, which had been sold to Nova Scotia in 1937; the *Frank A. Morey,* lost in the Bahamas in May, 1941; the *Leona & Marion,* lost in 1938; and the *Lillian E. Kerr,* built as a three-master in 1920, sold to Nova Scotia, rerigged with four masts, and run down and sunk by a steamer in 1942 with the loss of all hands. A big raised-deck three-master which used to operate along the coast to some extent was the *Ada Cliff,* built at Boothbay Harbor in 1918, although her name was changed within a year, and she became much better known by the name of *Frederick J. Lovatt.* None of these schooners was particularly attractive, having been built in the wartime boom when the construction of wooden vessels was becoming almost a lost art and when very little time or effort was wasted on such things as decoration or, in some cases, even good workmanship.

One possible exception to the foregoing was the *Lucy Evelyn,* a 374-ton three-master built in 1917 by Frye, Flynn & Co. at Harrington, Maine, for Captain E. C. Lindsay and the Machias Lumber Co. She was named for Captain Lindsay's two daughters, both of whom have passed away only in recent years. She cost $60,000

100. The *Edward R. Smith*, left high and dry by the tide at Lubec,
Maine. Captain F.E. Bowker photo, Mystic Seaport Museum.

ready for sea, and during her lifetime she must have earned it back several times over. For years she ran steadily to New York, taking lumber out and coming home with coal. She made good passages and kept out of serious trouble until her later years, but in 1933 she had a disastrous trip. The lumber and coal business being slack, her owners chartered her to load potatoes for New York. Sailing on February 22 she went outside, ran into a succession of westerly gales, and was blown almost across the Atlantic. Weeks later she turned up in Barbados with her cargo ruined and her crew exhausted and on the verge of starvation. After refitting at San Juan, Puerto Rico, she finally made New York on May 28, almost three months out. Coming home, she got ashore near Boothbay Harbor but the accident was not serious. In July, 1940, the *S. S. Yarmouth* of the Eastern Steamship Line plowed into her stern in a thick fog 30 miles south of Petit Manan. Captain John T. Irons got her back to Machiasport, where she was repaired, but he and the owners were about ready to call it quits. The captain retired in 1941, and she was sold to New York owners for $20,000.

She later became a Brava packet, carrying freight and passengers to the Cape Verde Islands, and when she became too poor even for that trade she was sold to become a tearoom and gift shop in New Jersey. She was taken down the coast, hauled into a permanent berth on one of the beaches, and there she lies today, awaiting the inevitable end.

Another equally familiar three-master was the much older *Rebecca R. Douglas* of 475 tons, built in 1894 by Kelley, Spear & Co. of Bath. She was a centerboarder, built for Philadelphia owners to operate in and out of the Delaware River and Chesapeake

101. The *Rebecca R. Douglas* with her long raised deck. Courtesy Roger C. Peterson.

102. The *Henry H. Chamberlain*—survivor of the "Portland Gale." Courtesy Captain W.J.L. Parker.

Bay. Until 1921, she was owned by the Franklin Baker Co. of Philadelphia and was commanded by Captain W. E. Ladd. She was engaged principally in the coconut trade from the Caribbean, and it was Captain Ladd who gave her the long, raised deck amidships. While this did not enhance her looks, it was a distinct asset in terms of increased carrying capacity. As long as he had the schooner, Captain Ladd always took his wife with him and they made their home aboard.

In 1921, the *Douglas* was sold to C. A. & B. F. Small Corp. of New York, owners of a number of other sailing vessels in the postwar years. She was registered in the name of one of the partners, Clarence Small, and hailed from Jonesport, Maine.

Prior to her purchase by them, she suffered the worst accident of her career, excepting her loss when, during a northeast gale, coming down over the Shoals through Pollock Rip Slue, she was rammed and sunk by the *S. S. Eastern Crown,* which struck her by the fore rigging and nearly cut her bow off. Captain J. W. Gay of Millbridge and his crew of six got away from her by the skin of their teeth, for she sank in less than three minutes. She was raised, however, and repaired and sailed under Small's ownership until 1932. She was then laid up for a long spell due to lack of business, but in 1937 Captain Burtis Wasson of Calais, former owner and master of the *Henry H. Chamberlain,* bought her and put her back into service. He managed to do well with her, but in 1943 he was ready to retire and sold her for a wartime price to New York owners. She was loaded and sailed for Barranquilla, Colombia, under command of Captain Walter Wrightson. Two days out of New York she ran into extremely bad weather and her aging seams opened up to such an extent she had to be abandoned. The crew got away from her before she sank, but the weather was so rough the boat capsized and the captain and all but two of the crew were drowned.

The *Henry H. Chamberlain,* a handy little three-master of 248 tons, was built at Phippsburg, Maine, in 1891 and had the unique distinction of being one of the few coasters to go to sea during the "Portland Gale" of 1898. It was very much of an involuntary sailing, for the *Chamberlain* had sought shelter just outside of Pemaquid Harbor, under the lee of the land and so confident of her safety were the captain and crew, that some of them went ashore to visit home. Two or three of the crew were still aboard when the gale struck, however, but they were helpless to do anything when her anchor chains parted, except try to steer her clear of the ledges between the schooner and open water. In this they were successful, but once at sea, there was nothing to do but let her run under bare poles before the gale. The schooner behaved nobly and weeks later crawled into port under her own canvas. Eventually, she came under the ownership of Captain Burt Wasson and was operated principally in the Calais lumber trade. She was eventually sold to Nova Scotia and is reported to have been lost about 1937.

Another little three-master of about the same vintage, the *Damietta & Joanna,* 314 tons, went offshore during the war and was lost in 1919 by stranding at Barbados, where she had put in on a voyage from Mobile to Point à Pitre.

The old *William D. Marvel,* of 432 tons, built away back in 1872 at Wilmington, Delaware, for the Taunton coal trade, arrived safely at Preston, England, in 1920 with a cargo of lumber from Sheet Harbor, Nova Scotia, only to catch fire when a drum of gasoline exploded. She was later condemned and broken up for firewood.

Another 1891 schooner, the 443-ton *Daisy Farlin,* also failed to survive the war by long. She had sailed from Port Arthur, Texas, bound for Tunis but opened up in heavy weather to such an extent she had to be abandoned. Her crew was picked up by the *S. S. Gulfmaid,* and within a few days they were back at their point of departure.

The 296-ton *Charles L. Jeffrey,* built in 1881, was sold to the Portuguese flag just after the war and renamed *Viajante.* She made only one voyage across, however, being lost at Santa Maria Island in the Cape Verdes in 1924.

The Thomaston three-master *E. Marie Brown,* of 456 tons, was lost toward the end of the war following a collision with the British steamer *Harmodious.* She took Captain Belyea and three of his seven-man crew down with her.

Built at Portsmouth, New Hampshire in 1886, the little 206-ton *Lizzie J. Call* always hailed from that port, although she operated most of the time with the Maine coasting fleet. She had been a handsome little schooner in her early days, being of a very fine model and had been noted as being the most "crooked" vessel on the coast, meaning she had a deeper sheer than others. She came out as a flush-decker but was rebuilt in her later years and given a raised quarterdeck. She also straightened out a lot in her old age and presented quite a different appearance than when she slid into the waters of the Piscataqua River more than thirty-five years be-

fore. She, too, was sold to the Portuguese in 1921 and disappeared from the registers shortly afterwards.

The *Emily F. Northam,* a three-master of 332 tons, built in Portland, Connecticut, in 1883, hailed from New York, although she ran down east for most of her career, and on her last trip, taking a load of coal down the coast, she got ashore near Cranberry Island. She was too badly damaged to be worth repairing so her cargo was removed and the hulk hauled into Cranberry Island Pool. There she was stripped by the islanders who eventually converted her into firewood. To get the masts out of her, they sawed channels through the deck and down the sides and pulled the spars out sideways.

One of the smallest three-masters in the later years was the *W. R. Perkins* of 178 tons, built at Millbridge in 1900 and hailing from Machias during most of her life on the coast. She ran steadily in the lumber trade until about the time of the First World War, when she was sold to go under Portuguese registry and renamed *Bemporath.* Still later, she became the *Genoveva,* hailing from Lisbon. I believe they kept her sailing for many years, trading from Portugal to the Azores and at last, according to report, to the lonely Cape Verdes.

The 374-ton *Thomas H. Lawrence,* built in Boston in 1891, was one of the last survivors of the type and was finally purchased for the Cape Verde packet trade. She had been familiar along the Maine coast for many years, and in the late thirties was laid up in Rockland. There, agents for the Cape Verde Islanders found her and bought her for a song. They hauled her on Snow's railway and had her caulked, painted, and refitted to some extent. Sailing

103. The *Thomas H. Lawrence* hauled on the Snow Shipyard railway. Hulk in the foreground is the *Annie B. Mitchell.* Larry Brown photo, in author's collection.

104. The *Thomas H. Lawrence* ashore at Ipswich. Larry Brown photo, in the author's collection.

for New Bedford to load for her first long traverse across the "middle passage" of the Atlantic, she got ashore at Ipswich, Massachusetts, and for a time it looked as though she would never even make her loading port. However, perseverance and high run of tides got her afloat once more and she continued on to New Bedford. She had been badly strained, however, and after sailing, she had to be towed back to port. It became apparent that she could never make the trans-Atlantic passage, so she was hauled onto a mudflat and abandoned.

Among other three-masters lost during or just after the First World War was the *Willie L. Maxwell,* built at Franklin, Maine, in 1896 and lost off South America in 1919. The little 213-ton *Leora M. Thurlow,* built at Bath in 1891 was sold to Key West, Florida, and was lost in the Caribbean in 1920.

The decrepit old lumber drogher *St. Croix,* built at Calais in 1866, was lost during the twenties as was the *F. H. Odiorne,* one of the last schooners built at Newburyport, Massachusetts. The stormy Atlantic also accounted for the Rockport-built *Adelia T. Carleton* and the beautiful *Carrie E. Look,* which went missing with her eight-man crew.

The old Bangor River schooner *Melissa Trask,* which had the dubious distinction of being the homeliest three-master on the coast, survived a severe stranding to be sold to the Portuguese, but she did not last too long afterward.

Typical of many schooners built along the Connecticut shore and brought east in later years was the smart-looking and well-kept *Fannie & Fay,* of Machias. She was launched at New London in 1885, but was shortly afterward sold to Maine and thereafter

105. The *Fannie & Fay* at Machias, loading lumber. Courtesy Charles
S. Morgan.

ran steadily in the Machias–New York lumber trade. Her master for many years was Captain William Sanborn of Machias, who, with other members of his family, owned many of her shares. He had previously been in the two-master *Regina* when she was still owned in Machias, and after leaving the coasting trade, he became widely known as the operator of the little combination tug and water boat *Ben Hur,* a fixture in Portland Harbor. The *Fanny & Fay* also went South about the time of the first war and foundered off the Dry Tortugas about 1925. She was then reported to be under the command of Captain Lonnie Murphy, formerly a protégé of Captain Arthur Stevens of the *Alice S. Wentworth.*

Machias was always the home port of some fine vessels, and the *Sawyer Brothers* was no exception. Of 374 tons, she was built at Millbridge and named for her owners, who also had the *D. J. Sawyer,* the *Frances Sawyer,* the *Grand Turk,* and several others.

One little three-master with a similar name but from a different part of the coast, was the 284-ton *Nellie F. Sawyer,* built at Brunswick, Maine, as far back as 1873. She was remembered primarily, however, because of her master, Captain Dan Willard of Portland, who was in her until he was seventy-eight years old. He was called "Yankee Dan" and bore a remarkable resemblance to Abraham Lincoln. For many years he was the guest of honor at the annual banquet of the Lincoln Club of Portland, where his resemblance to the Great Emancipator caused many guests attending for the first time to think they were seeing a ghost.

The foregoing does not begin to include all the three-masted schooners under Maine registry in those last years of the trade, but it does include some of the more notable ones that were familiar along the coast and the discharging wharves of Boston and New York.

By the midthirties, the number of schooners of any rig had diminished almost to the vanishing point, although as mentioned previously, the two-masted *Endeavor* was built at Deer Isle as late as 1938.

The Second World War gave the *coup-de-grâce* to the coasting trade, and the few old veterans that had clung to the last dropped away, until suddenly there was not one left. Except for the bright canvas of an occasional yacht or a dude cruise schooner, not a sail could be seen where for more than 200 years they had been sighted daily from every Maine headland. The little communities which had grown up looking eagerly seaward, now seemed to turn their faces inland, leaving the bays, rivers, and wide expanses of coastal water to the few fishermen who follow their calling in powerful motorboats.

The era of sail has gone, giving place to science and the quickened pulse of the present, but to many who saw and knew them, the passing of these old vessels and the resourceful men who sailed them is tinged with sadness. In another decade or so, there will be no memory to bring back the cough of the donkey engine, the rattle of anchor chain, and the thundering of wind-filled canvas; none to remember the leaning spars and the bellying topsails against the blue sky or the looming of ghostly hulls through the fog. The old schooners will have passed into maritime history in company with the stately galleon, the swift clipper, and the giant down-east Cape Horners, their only distinction that of having closed the era of commercial sail in America.

GLOSSARY

Becket — A piece of line, usually about ½ inch diameter, length to suit, with an eye splice in one end large enough to slip over a spoke of the steering wheel and the other end spliced or knotted into an eye in the deck beneath the wheel. Usually there were two of them. Some blocks also have what is termed a becket, meaning a fitting on the heel of the block into which the standing part of a fall is spliced.

Bo's'n's chair — A seat consisting of a board about 8 to 10 inches wide, 24 to 30 inches long and 1 to 1½ inches thick. Holes about 1 inch in diameter are bored through each corner and a length of line is passed through to form a bridle with a double eye into which a hook can be inserted. The chair is used to hoist a man aloft so he can work with his hands free.

Box rail — A closed-in or solid rail as opposed to an open, or fly, rail, around the edge of the quarterdeck or poop, sometimes extending part or all of the way forward.

Bricker — A schooner, invariably two-masted, designed and built to carry brick cargoes. Brickers were wide of beam and shoal draft, hardly more than sailing lighters, and carried the largest part of their cargo on deck. Most of them were built around the Hudson River, although a few originated in New England.

Bucko — Any ship's officer who was prone to enforce his orders by liberal use of his fists, belaying pin, or any other weapon handy.

Buffalo rail — A low solid rail forward or aft on a schooner. Forward it extended from the knightheads aft on top of the main rail to about the fore rigging. The catheads projected outboard through it and the fluke of the anchor hooked over it. Aft it usually served as a sill on which the fly rail stanchions were mounted.

Bull's-eye — A kind of small single-holed deadeye of lignum vitae, scored around the perimeter to take a lashing. It is used primarily as a fairleader for running rigging. A *lizard* is similar but is usually smaller and customarily suspended from a *pennant* — a piece of line, long or short, which is spliced around the lizard, the other end being made fast to a spar or stay where necessary.

Carvel planked — Smooth-sided boats, differentiated from *lap streak* or *clinker-built* boats in which the edge of one plank laps over the next one below it.

Chance along — With a fair wind blowing and weather conditions favorable, coastermen spoke of having "a *chance along.*"

Clew up — To take in a topsail by letting go tack and sheet and lastly the halyard while also hauling on the clewline which gathers the sail into a bunch at the masthead. It is then necessary for someone to climb aloft and furl it, folding the sail in more neatly and lashing it to the masthead with gaskets.

Coach house — A small auxiliary structure like a vestibule through which the after house is entered from the main deck.

Coaster — Any vessel carrying cargo from one coastal port to another. A few coasters carried cargoes to and from the West Indies but none were considered deep water vessels. In this country the coasting trade was carried on almost entirely in sailing vessels.

Companionway — A stairway leading down from the deck to living quarters, whether in after cabin or forecastle (if the latter is below decks).

Crib wharf — A common type of wharf construction down east. Logs are laid out in a square pattern from the shore much as they would be in a log cabin but not as deeply notched. The square is then filled with rocks and dirt.

Document — The government certificate or paper which lists the size and tonnage of a vessel, date of building, list of owners, and name of the master. It is the legal identification record of the vessel and has to be renewed every year or at any time when an alteration is made to hull or rig or when there is any change of ownership in whole or in part.

Donkey's breakfast — A seaman's mattress — a bag of ticking roughly 2½ feet by 6 feet, filled with straw.

Down east — From New York to Canada, along the coast, sailing coasters have always been bound *down east* when headed toward Maine or Nova Scotia. The commonest explanation of the term is that the winds are generally more favorable for a ship headed in that direction, going *down wind*. Sailing from Maine or Nova Scotia, one goes *up to the west'ard*.

Drogher — Name often applied to vessels that customarily carried heavy bulk cargoes.

Dude cruisers — Former coasting schooners refitted to carry passengers on pleasure cruises.

Fly rail — An open rail enclosing the quarterdeck or poop or extending forward as far as the raised quarterdeck may be carried. It was usually 1 to 2 feet high and was set on turned wooden stanchions spaced fore and aft about 3 or 4 feet apart.

Foot blocks — Large closed blocks through which the hauling part of the halyards was led to the winch heads, through one or more snatch blocks to insure a fair lead.

Fush out — A down-east expression which means to die out, as the wind does at times, creating a calm.

Gaff — A spar to which the head or top of a quadrilateral fore and aft sail was laced.

Gasket — Long or short pieces of line used to tie up sails furled at mastheads or bowsprits.

Gear — Used as a general term for all lines or equipment necessary to set, trim, or take in sails or for equipment used for some other particular purpose.

Gunkhole — Down-east name for a tidal inlet or basin, not a real harbor. There are many such along the 2,500-mile Maine coast. The word has been adopted in late years by cruising yachtsmen who seek out these secluded and usually delightful anchorages and who call the search *gunkholing*.

Halyards — Lines rove off (led) through blocks to hoist any sail to its full extent up the mast. The *throat halyard* was that fastened to the inner end of the gaff nearest the mast. The *peak halyards* were fast to the outer end of the gaff. These halyards consisted of several parts but *jib halyards* were usually single or, at the most, double.

Hand — Any man serving as an ordinary or able-bodied seaman or any man not an officer.

Hand puller — A coasting schooner not having a hoisting engine, and in which all sails and anchor gear were manipulated by hand.

Hatch coamings — Heavy timbers, mortised into each other at the ends, which surround the hatch opening and extend 6 to 12 inches above the deck level. Hatch covers are placed on them to prevent water from getting below decks.

Hawse pipes — Flanged iron pipes through the bow, through which passes the chain from windlass to anchor.

Headsails — All triangular sails set before the foremast. The innermost headsail on any coaster is called the *jib* if it sets on a stay which runs from the masthead to the end of the bowsprit. The next one out is called the *flying jib* and if there is one further out, it is the *outer jib,* contrary to the practice common in deep water ships. If the innermost sail is set on a stay which extends from foremast head to stem head, it is called a *fore staysail.* Such a rig is usually found only in larger coasters and in fishermen where it is called a *jumbo.*

H'ister — Down-east name for the *hoisting,* or *donkey, engine.* This machine is usually located near the foremast, is gasoline powered, water cooled, and is equipped with at least two winch heads for hoisting sails and cargo, and is often hooked up in various ingenious ways to the anchor windlass and pumps.

Hogged — An old schooner is said to be hogged when, instead of her rail line curving upward, forward, and aft, she is humped in the middle, as though she were going to break in two.

In a vessel — Among coastermen, no one ever sails *on* a vessel, nor even *aboard* a vessel. One sails or goes *in* a vessel and is only aboard when the vessel is at anchor or at a wharf.

In company — When two or more vessels are sailing within sight of each other, they are said to be *in company.* Often when discussing a vessel, someone might say, "I've never been in her but I've sailed in company with her."

Jibboom — In small coasters, a boom to which the foot of the jib is made fast is the *jibboom,* and the *flying jibboom* is the spar which extends outboard on top of the bowsprit, although speaking casually, it also is often referred to as the *jibboom.*

Knightheads — Timbers projecting upward through the deck, one at each side of the stem. The bowsprit extends outboard between them. In ancient days, the tops of these timbers were carved to represent knight's heads — hence the name.

Lazarette — In a coaster, the space under the quarterdeck entered through a small hatch, usually hinged, abreast of the wheel box and used for the storage of spare gear and sails, etc.

Leech — The after edge of a fore and aft sail or the leeward edge of a square sail when she is on the wind. The upper edge of any sail is always the *head* and the lower edge is the *foot.* The windward or weather edge is the *luff.*

Light — Vessel with little or no cargo aboard. To be *flying light* means to be in the best sailing trim possible, usually with no cargo whatsoever.

Missing stays — *Staying* in this case is synonymous with *tacking. Missing stays* simply means the vessel failed to tack.

Nothin' to or *nothin' off* — For instance, if the course is *southeast by south* and the order is given as "nothin' to," any deviation from the given course should be away from the basic course or to the southward. If the order is "nothin' off," any deviation allowed should be toward the southeast.

Overhaul — A rope or chain is *overhauled* when it is pulled clear in such fashion that it does not restrain whatever it is attached to. The opposite is to *take it in* or *set it up;* i.e., to tighten it again.

Pays off — The vessel turns away from the wind and picks up speed as the wind fills the sails.

Pennant (originally *pendant*) — A length of rope, wire, or chain used to suspend a block from a masthead, yardarm, or from some point on the hull. The Spanish burton anchor tackle was hung from a pennant which was made fast at the foremast head; the boom tackles were usually hooked into pennants which were shackled into eyes in the rail just aft of the next set of rigging forward; the foot blocks were shackled to chain pennants to bring aboard a deckload of lumber; and jib sheet blocks were at the end of pennants from the clew of any loose-footed jibs.

Rap full — When a vessel has tacked and swings off the wind and her sails are as full as they can be without luffing, she is said to have a *rap full*. The order is then "keep her full and by" meaning to keep her by the wind with sails trimmed close without shaking.

Reaches — Waterways along the coast with sufficient depth of water to permit sailing vessels to operate. Usually these are bounded by the mainland on one side and islands or shoal areas on the other.

"Riz" deck (raised deck) — A vessel in which the main or weather deck has been carried forward at the height of the main rail. In larger schooners, the deck was often carried all the way forward to the knightheads with the windlass and heel of the bowsprit below deck. In smaller schooners the deck usually extended only to the foremast, leaving a short well deck in the bow for the windlass and bowsprit heel.

Seizings — Lashing of marline used when stays or other standing rigging are turned back on themselves to form an eye, instead of being spliced. There are *flat seizings, round seizings, throat seizings,* and so forth.

She died — When a vessel was hauled into some cove or backwater and was stripped and abandoned, she was left to *die*. Some areas, such as a section of Tenant's Harbor, Maine, were spoken of as *schooner graveyards* because they were favorite places to abandon worn out vessels.

Shrouds — Rope in the early days and wire in the later years, which guyed the lower masts and topmasts transversely. The shrouds that guyed the masts fore and aft were called *stays* and were included in the general term of *standing rigging*.

Snatch blocks — Blocks made so that they can be opened at the side to allow a line to be inserted and can be hooked into eye bolts in the deck or elsewhere to insure a fair lead to the winch heads for hoisting. A *fair lead* is a line led so that it does not chafe.

Spitting her caulking — Old vessels have a way of *working* under sail, and the oakum with which the seams are caulked may work out, particularly in ships whose seams have become so hollow from long years of caulking and recaulking that the oakum cannot be driven or packed in solidly. *Oakum* is shredded-up hemp thoroughly impregnated with tar which is packed into the seams to make the vessel tight.

Spring stay — The stay which extends from one masthead to another in all fore and aft schooners.

Standing rigging — Any rope, wire, or chain which affords support to masts, bowsprit, etc., as opposed to *running rigging* which controls sails, etc., usually operating through blocks.

Stopper — A length of line, usually equivalent in diameter to the size of the halyard, made fast to the shackle of the foot block and wrapped around the hauling part of a halyard in a rolling hitch and several round turns. Once the halyard was cast off the winch head, it could be held with one hand while the other hand turned it around a belaying pin.

Suck — *To get a suck* means to pump a vessel dry enough so that the pumps suck air, the noise indicating that all the water is out.

Tack — The lower forward corner of any fore and aft sail. On a topsail tack designates not only the lower corner of the sail but also the line which controls it. It also means the maneuver made by a schooner when she beats to windward, swinging alternately from one side of the course to the other so the wind can fill the sails on one side and the other alternately.

Tail rope — Ropes led from the clew of the jib to each pin rail forward, leading down through a bull's-eye seized to each forward shroud and thence to a belaying pin.

Thoroughfares — Channels or waterways between islands, particularly in the Penobscot Bay area. Similar to *reaches* but not directly adjacent to the mainland.

Tons or *tonnage* — A measurement based on an arbitrary formula, intended originally to be a rough measure of cargo capacity. Tonnage has nothing to do with displacement or the like.

Two blocks — A sail is said to be *two blocks* when it is hoisted as far as it will go, or when any two blocks in a tackle (pronounced *tay*ckle) are brought as close together as possible.

Two-topmaster — Designating any two-masted schooner with two topmasts aloft. There were also *one-topmasters* and *bald-headers,* the latter being vessels which carried no topmasts at all.

U bolt — A bolt shaped as the name implies whose *legs* are extended through the deck, rails, beams, or other timbers and are fastened on the under side with nuts over washers or clinch rings. One exception to this is the U bolt thrust downward into holes in the barrel of a windlass to act as a guide for the anchor chain and to prevent overriding turns.

Voyage — No coasting schooner makes a coastal voyage. She makes a *trip* or a *passage.* She may make a voyage to the West Indies and back but many hands and skippers would still refer to it as a *trip.*

Watch tackle — A small tackle made up with two double blocks and used to steady a main boom or haul it to windward or to make standing rigging taut.

Well deck — A main deck below the level of the main rail. It may extend from the poop forward or it may extend only far enough aft from the bow to include the inboard length of the bowsprit, the samson post, the windlass, chain boxes, and so forth.

Winch heads — Flared drums at each end of a shaft operated by the hoisting engine or sometimes by cranks only at the base of a mast. Halyards are wound around them in order to apply power to hoist sails, cargo, or for any other purpose.

Windlass — A device for taking in the anchor chain. It is mounted horizontally. On a *log windlass,* the chain passes around the barrel of the windlass in three round turns and on the *wildcat model,* the chain passes over the barrel, the links being engaged by a notched casting into which they fit. Most smaller and older coasters used a log windlass operated by hand brakes or handles hooked to ratchet ring gears on the barrels of the windlass.

Wung out (winged out) — Also spoken of as being *wing and wing.* A two-masted schooner with the wind coming from dead astern usually tries to keep the mainsail broad off on one side and the foresail on the other. Larger schooners also tried to alternate their sails but if there was room, a multimasted schooner would often *tack down wind* bringing the wind first over one quarter and then over the other to enable all sails to draw well and yet equalize the course sailed.

VESSEL INDEX

W. D. Mangam —- 71
W. R. Perkins — 192
Wasp — 172*, 176
Wawenock — 187
Westway — 167
Whiteway — 167
William Bisbee — 159*, 160
William Booth — 60, 159, 170, 173
William C. Pendleton — 112, 113*, 145, 146
William D. Marvel — 191, 192
William H. Jewell — 45, 47

William H. Waters — 168
William Keene — 138, 143*
Willie L. Maxwell — 128*, 194
William P. Boggs — 149
Witch Hazel — 179, 180*
Wyoming — 170

Yankee Girl — 160
Yankee Star — 161

This second volume in the American Maritime Library

WAKE OF THE COASTERS

has been composed in Linotype Garamond and reprinted by offset lithography by Eastern Press, Inc. The paper is Mohawk Superfine. Binding by the Mueller Trade Bindery, Inc.